To Ron —
Best regards

Bob H.H.

i

Sir Allen & Me

An insider's look
at R. Allen Stanford
and the island
of Antigua

Published by
Southern Cross Publications
PO Box 24704
Christiansted
US Virgin Islands
00824
southerncrosspubs@gmail.com

ISBN: 978-0-692-00443-2

Published in the United States of America

Cover design by Michael Baron

Antigua map courtesy of antiguanice.com

For Keva

R.I.P.

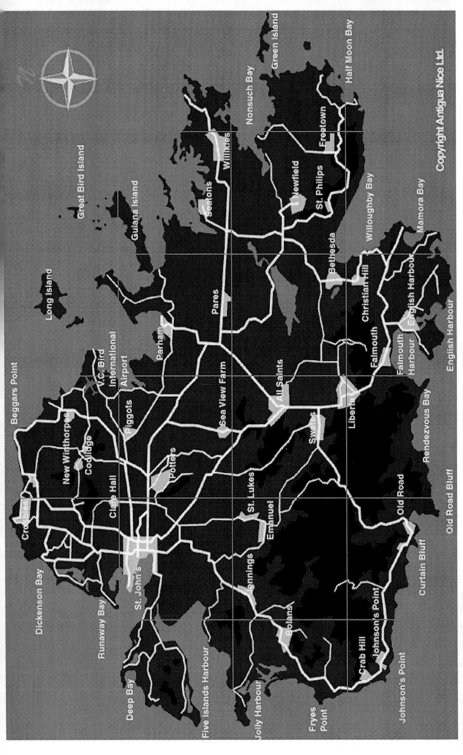

Table of Contents

1
The Crash

When, on February 17, 2009, the financial empire of Texas billionaire R. Allen Stanford collapsed, the consequences for thousands of people in dozens of countries were appalling. Careers were interrupted and in some cases ruined. Investors who had been promised the world found themselves grasping for vapors. Stanford's close associates faced years on the bad side of prison bars. The government of the West Indian island nation of Antigua & Barbuda went into shock, as hundreds of its citizens and foreign residents were abruptly unemployed.

On St. Croix in the United States Virgin Islands scores of folks – lured by Stanford's move to that jurisdiction in 2007 as he crooned his familiar financial siren song, many of whom having given up good jobs elsewhere at good salaries – were left stranded with newly bought homes and deracinated families. Small businesses on both islands suddenly faced bankruptcy after piling up inventories and engaging workers to satisfy the orders and contracts with the Texan's companies and employees. A fixed-base operation at the St. Croix airport that had been fueling Stanford's business jets saw a drop of $50,000 a month in revenue. A furniture store in the main town of

Christiansted found itself stuck with merchandise ordered by Stanford employees who had precipitously evaporated.

For me, and for many others like me who, we felt, had been at one point or another treated shabbily and often cruelly by Stanford and his various hatchet men and women, The Crash imbued us with a sense of elevated *schadenfreude*, a personal delight over the denouement of Stanford's Greek tragedy finally being played out.

The man's tragic flaw, which Aristotle described as the protagonist's fatal mistake, was Stanford's vaunted sense of self. In Tom Wolfe's memorable term in "Bonfire of the Vanities," Stanford was a Master of the Universe, at least in his own head. Events conspired, as in Wolfe's novel, to undo our hero in a spectacular reversal brought on by hubris and a false sense of unassailability.

But my glow of *schadenfreude* was fairly short-lived. I began to feel a little, but not very, sorry for Stanford. He was also a victim, even if he had no one else to blame.

He started life in the little Texas town of Mexia (pop. 7,000). Robert Allen Stanford's grandfather, Lodis, had been a barber and had started up an insurance agency during the Great Depression in Mexia. Allen's father James took over running the insurance agency after World War II and renamed it Stanford Financial.

Allen was born in 1950. When he was nine years old, his parents divorced and Robert Allen, his brother and mother moved to Fort Worth.

At Baylor University, he majored in finance, no doubt dreaming that someday he'd be fairly prosperous. At six-feet-four and obsessed with physical fitness, he was good-looking, persuasive and nakedly ambitious. From his graduation from college up until the The Crash, when federal investigators nailed him to the cross he himself designed, Stanford had climbed to heady altitudes. Listed in *Forbes*' 2008 richest-Americans club as the 205th wealthiest person in the nation with a net worth of something like $2.2 billion, R. Allen (no mere Robert now) was looking a lot like a Master of the Universe. Alas, on that catastrophic day in February 2009, it was all suddenly gone with the wind. And gone was his name from *Forbes*, unmentioned in the 2009 richest–Americans issue.

Along the way, his life and mine crossed. For two years he was my boss, in Antigua, from 1996 until late 1998. I have never met, and I hope never to meet again, a man so engaging and terrifying all at once. An observant, more or less, Baptist, Stanford could show what appeared to be genuine compassion for the less-well-heeled among us. Yet he was also capable of brutally humiliating his managers and even his closest friends, like Stanford Financial Group CFO James (Jim) Davis, in the presence of others, often at meetings (maybe that should be "audiences"). His fuse was short, and he was pretty certifiably paranoid. He was noted for suddenly slamming his open hand hard down on the table to make his point more clearly understood. He thought he was being spied on by the British intelligence agency MI6, and he once sent me off to Trinidad to look into the doings of a British man he suspected of using the cover of an offshore financial expert to nose into Stanford's private business. He accused one of his employees, me, of starting up a business in another Antilles island (entirely false), suggesting some sort of skullduggery was afoot to undermine him. That most of his suspicions were easily dismissed as fantasies was not a consideration. Stanford was not as interested in reality as he was in the indivisible importance of the Master. As one old Antigua native nicely put it: "Stanford's penis, dat's his checkbook, and he screw eva'body in da worl'."

It's easy enough to say in retrospect, but when I first met him in an interview in his Houston company's opulent offices in 1996 I had an strange impression, a vague suspicion, that what I was seeing was not as advertised. What set me thinking was his face. Somewhere after his adolescence, Stanford decided to grow a moustache. This was another of his missteps. As a substitution for head hair, men often grow beards. Moustaches are more difficult to analyze.

It made him look ... *phony*. But who could argue against these elegant offices we were in, gleaming with burnished mahogany and dark shiny leather? Who could argue that the suit my interviewer was wearing was not

4

worth at least $3,000, that the private jet he referred to was not worth around $35 million, that the abject obeisance paid him by his underlings came not from fear but affection? Who could argue that this guy was not real, and maybe not even rich? No one would sanely entertain such notions. What I did not know at the time was that Allen's vast fortune was nearly all other people's money. And he was spending it accordingly.

What R. Allen Stanford yearned for since his boyhood in Mexia and Fort Worth was *class.* Like The Great Gatsby, he was trying to get from new-money West Egg to old-money East Egg, to be accepted into the storied circles of the Upper Class. Stanford labored under the perennial delusion that class could be purchased. Most Texas millionaires or billionaires don't worry about a little horseshit on their boots or having a burger at Dairy Queen, but that was not Stanford's style. He wanted to be noticed, to make an impression, to have his inferiors groveling at his feet, to buy and wear and drive and fly and hire The Best. His office walls were hung with prints (they might have been original oils) of English hunting scenes, with the hounds and the horses and the riding helmets, the British social cream at play. He wanted people to think he was blood-related to Leland Stanford, the founder of Stanford University in 1885. The school had accepted Allen's donation of $2.5 million toward the refurbishment of Leland Stanford's home in 2006 but later wound up bringing suit against the Texan for improperly invoking a lineage that did not exist. Leland Stanford was a major Robber Baron, one of the fat-cat capitalists of his day, like Carnegie, Astor, Rockefeller and Morgan. Robber Barons were considered by their detractors of having amassed great fortunes through dodgy business practices, tyrannical management and financial scamming. Little wonder that R. Allen Stanford held his non-relative Leland as a possible role model.

Allen even managed to become knighted. According to the account of this distinction by Stanford's publicists, on November 1, 2006, he was "appointed Knight Commander of the Most Distinguished Order of the Nation [Antigua & Barbuda]. He was presented this honor by the Governor-General of that island nation, Sir James B. Carlisle, in a ceremony attended by His Royal Highness Prince Edward, Earl of Wessex, in celebration of the country's Silver Jubilee.

"A deeply honored Stanford said, 'My love for the Caribbean, its people and future, particularly that of Antigua and Barbuda, has been clearly displayed by my commitment to the region over the past two decades through long-term investment of capital and human resources.

" 'It is my hope that the grant of this great personal honor is a reflection of that commitment. I truly hope that this appointment will increase awareness of the success that the Stanford companies have achieved with Caricom

[Caribbean Community] nationals comprising the vast majority of our employee base, and that it will further promote the economic and social development of the region.' " Prince Edward, one might venture, had no idea then who the hell R. Allen Stanford was, but he does now.

Stanford's pretense to class was further underscored by his much-broadcast involvement in cricket, golf and – of course – polo. No Joe Sixpack here, rooting for the Cowboys. Stanford was into *cricket*, that quintessentially British gentlemen's sport, impenetrably wrapped in arcane rules that few Americans and surely no Texan can ever fathom. One writer said, "Cricket makes baseball look like jacks." His audacious helicopter descent into the hallowed Lord's Cricket Ground in London to promote his equally audacious Twenty20 match series brought a torrent of guffaws from the English cricket pundits, who knew full well that Stanford didn't know any more about cricket than he did about quantum physics. Alighting from the rented chopper, Stanford gave waiting dignitaries a big Texas hug and flashed a Plexiglas box he proclaimed held $20 million in cash. This was ostensibly the prize money to go to the winners of his first Stanford Twenty20 cricket match to be played in Antigua between the English team and the Stanford Superstars, an *ad hoc* squad cobbled together from the best West Indian players. The English cricket community was aghast. In the event, the Stanford team obliterated the English squad, and each of the Superstars presumably walked away with just under a million dollars each. Some left their winnings with Stanford International Bank. Sir Allen assured them the money would be safe.

Anyone wishing to make the case that Sir Allen was an unrepentant narcissist need not look further than Antigua. As an arriving passenger stepped out of the terminal at the V.C. Bird International Airport, he could take in, clockwise from his left, Stanford Cricket Ground and his Sticky Wicket restaurant; Stanford Trust Company; Stanford International Bank; his up-market Pavilion restaurant; and just down the road, Stanford Development Company. Behind some trees a low, long blue building housed the *Antigua Sun* and Sun Printing & Publishing, the companies I was hired to start up in 1996. These were real buildings, but they were also a kind of financial Potemkin Village – Sir Allen's egregious and laughable sinkholes of other people's money. As a former Stanford International Bank accountant told me after The Crash, "Not a single one of Stanford's businesses in Antigua made a profit. Every dime was extracted from the offshore bank," including the money to pay for his posh lifestyle. "When I questioned this," the accountant said, "he fired me."

Sir Allen also more or less hijacked the already famous Antigua Sailing Week, which for four decades has drawn sailing yachts from around the globe for racing and partying and showing off. Stanford put up some money to promote the annual event, and presto, it became Stanford Antigua Sailing Week. And back in Houston, Stanford Development Corporation had built a 40-unit condominium complex in 2002, called ... Stanford Lofts. Five years later, the condo owners association filed a construction-defect lawsuit against the building's developers, charging Stanford Development with "breach of contract, breach of warranty, fraud, negligent design, construction and supervision," according to the on-line Swamplot realty newsletter. Seems the building was physically falling apart, and the condos, which cost from $250,000 to $500,000, were essentially unsalable at anywhere near those prices by the owners.

That was another surprise for those who knew the man. Because, in Stanford's world, *everything* had to be "the best of the best," his own words. He hired, generally, exceedingly capable people. The architecture of his buildings, like the Georgian dignity of Stanford International Bank itself, was arresting and exquisite, conveying an aura of solidity and success. The landscaping around the bank was breathtaking, with cascading bougainvillea, exotic cacti, bursting clusters of ferns and stately royal palms. His business jets were private aviation's top-tier aircraft: two Gulfstream IVs, a Bombardier Global Express, and three or four smaller but still stunningly expensive Hawkers. One of his Stanford Aviation employees told a reporter that Stanford's private-jet fleet was "the largest in the world." Utter nonsense, to be sure, but that's what he probably believed since that's what Stanford probably told him. It hard to comprehend how many lies and evasions and facades Stanford visited on so many people.

If you worked for Stanford, your dress code included a gold Stanford shield with a stylized profile of The Stanford Eagle, his mascot and logo, pinned to your lapel, and it had to be affixed at the proper angle, not tilted or, God forbid, upside-down. This was your symbol of commitment and faith, and anyone who showed up without his or her pin was in for it. At an early meeting of my staff at the *Antigua Sun* newspaper in 1997, he cleared the air: "Here are your priorities: God, family and Allen Stanford – in that order."

I got the feeling I had made a grave mistake.

2
From riches to rags

In 1996, when I first shook hands with R. Allen Stanford in his Houston office complex, I was bankrupt. After many years of freelance journalism, writing magazine articles, book reviews and op-ed essays, along with my wife Lesley and my closest friend Paul Schmitt I had opened a restaurant in Hermosa Beach, California, in 1982 on borrowed money. After two years of sleepless nights and 15-hour days, we had paid back the loans, and Martha's 22nd Street Grill had become among the most popular breakfast-and-lunch eateries in the South Bay. Paul was the chef, and his menu was a triumph of imagination and uncompromising taste. The place was packed every day, and we were raking in money as I had never imagined possible for an old black-coffee-and-Camels journalist like me. We bought a struggling Mexican restaurant next door and broke down the wall, adding a prep kitchen and forty more setups.

The work was long and arduous, but the rewards were commensurate. We bought a house in the San Bernardino Mountains to escape to a few days a week (rotating between Lesley and me as managers at the store), a new car, make that two new cars, and we had bags of money.

By the late 1980s, we were all a bit burned out and weary of the routine. When we got an offer to sell the business, it was not a difficult decision. We made the deal, moved to our Big Bear Lake five-bedroom, three-bath mountainside house. Our net worth, I announced modestly one morning to Lesley, was just under one million dollars.

It took me five years to lose every nickel, but I managed to pull it off.

The two rental houses we bought, the weekly newspaper we started up and the purchase of the building we published it from, all seemed like sound moves to me, the brilliant restaurateur and noted writer.

But there was one aspect I failed to take into consideration: We lived in California. On June 28, 1992, at 8:05 in the morning, a 6.4-magnitude earthquake, whose epicenter was five miles from our verandah (technically, an aftershock of the Landers 7.3 quake three hours earlier), took just over 10 seconds to wipe us out.

Real estate values dropped 30 percent, and all our mortgages went under water. Advertising in our *Bear Valley Voice* newspaper, which was weak to begin with, evaporated.

The entire rear wall of the paper's building fell to the ground, leaving our offices and newsroom with a fine view of the lake and forests and distant mountains.

A wiser man would have conceded defeat. I was not that man. We borrowed from relatives, ran up the credit cards, let the mortgages on the rental homes go unpaid, and hit up the Small Business Administration for "relief." We bailed out of the newspaper building and defaulted on the mortgage (held by its former owners), moving operations to rented and much smaller digs in the City of Big Bear Lake. We were staying afloat, but we were treading water and gradually running out of buoyancy.

We filed for personal bankruptcy in the fall of 1994. We got to keep our cars and household furniture, but not much else. Bankruptcy is an experience I would not wish on my most fervent enemy, by the way. Even so, it lets you get up and started again, albeit with no credit and no cash. We were able to limp along for a couple more years. Yet we knew it was impossible to get back on our feet in Big Bear Lake, to get up and get started again.

Our exit strategy was leaning toward a return to Los Angeles, where Lesley was all but guaranteed to find work in the movie and television business. She had helped produce feature movies and television series for years before the restaurant venture, and Hollywood is an easy place to get a job as long as you know somebody, and she certainly did.

For my part, I could go back to freelancing for magazines and newspapers, maybe write a book on how to lose a million dollars.

"Look at this," Lesley said one morning, waving a copy of *Editor & Publisher*. "There's a classified looking for someone to start up a newspaper in the islands."

"What islands?"

"Doesn't say."

Nantucket and Martha's Vineyard came to mind. But in my depressed state, I thought it unlikely that we suddenly got lucky. Still, the job qualifications fit us nearly perfectly.

"Sounds too good to be true," Lesley said. "Nobody ever gets those jobs that are too good to be true."

I agreed, and Lesley tossed the magazine aside. A couple of weeks later, I decided I had nothing to lose but the postage to apply for the "islands" job, and if I failed at least Lesley's maxim about being too good would be verified. I sent off the package, along with copies of the *Bear Valley Voice*, to a box at the magazine, the advertiser obviously choosing to remain, for the moment, anonymous. About three weeks passed. I had almost forgotten about the matter. Then one morning the phone rang with a woman named Margaret Stein on the line. She identified herself as the human resources director for a company called Stanford Financial Group in Houston. The job, she said, was in the Caribbean island of Antigua. Was I familiar with it?

Oh, yeah. Antigua. Oh, sure. In the Caribbean. I knew all about it. Indeed, I said, I used to fly private charters around the Caribbean in the sixties, which was true, if you think the Bahamas are in the Caribbean, which they aren't, and also happen to be about 1,100 miles north of Antigua. Nonetheless, it seemed good enough for Margaret Stein.

"Can you fly to Houston for an interview?"

I allowed as to the possibility, as my heart moved further up my throat. The Lord had taken away, and now it looked like He was about to give it back.

"Absolutely," I said.

A few days later, a taxi delivered us to a small hotel steps from the headquarters of Stanford Financial Group, across Westheimer Street from the sprawling Galleria shopping center in Houston. The company operated out of a sturdy, multi-story, block-long modern complex that radiated a no-nonsense, solid, lots-of-money-inside quality. I was impressed. Whoever this guy R. Allen Stanford was, by whom we were about to be interviewed, he was loaded, even by Texas traditions.

At nine o'clock the next morning we presented ourselves at Stanford Financial Group reception and were asked to cool our heels on in a room lined with burnished hardwood paneling hung with English hunting scenes. We were eventually escorted to the human resources offices, and pre-interviewed not by Ms. Stein, who was out of town, but a delightful woman named Alice who seemed genuinely dazzled over all the things we had done in our lives. (She didn't hear the half of it.) And then off to Mr. Stanford's office along a corridor with a tall glass wall, on the other side of which sat scores of well-appointed people who appeared to be conducting their important business in satisfied earnest.

Mr. Stanford, big and impeccably dressed, welcomed us to Houston and so on, and we took our seats on a plush, low leather sofa. He asked us mostly softball questions, queried Alice if a background check had been done, which I thought a bit odd since the answer would necessarily have been yes. At that moment a young woman came in bearing a tray with a bottle of beet juice or some other health drink and some pills. She set the tray on Stanford's desk. Without a word he spun around with his back toward us and tossed the contents of the bottle into his mouth and downed some pills. He turned back around to face us, with no apologies for any perceived rudeness, but obviously unaware that he was now sporting a beetroot moustache.

"Get Laurence up here," he barked at Alice, who was hovering in the background.

Laurence turned out to be Laurence Arevalo, the young Stanford chief computer technician. He soon appeared and took a seat, asking us what sort of computer system we might need – if we were to actually get the job. I said it didn't matter to me whether we had Macs or PCs, but I would prefer a Microsoft NT machine as a server. Stanford wrinkled his brow.

"You can talk about computers later. I don't know anything about that."

Question was: Why did he call Laurence into his office if he didn't want to listen to computer lingo? Answer presumably was: He wanted to see if I knew what I was talking about.

"I want you to fly down to Antigua and see if you think you could live there," Stanford said. To Alice he said: "Check the airlines and see when the next plane leaves."

"But, Mr. Stanford," I said, "we have to go back to California and put out our paper. Can we go next week?'

"OK. As soon as possible. By the way, I want you to understand that I will be exercising no editorial control over the paper's content. All I expect is that it will be head-and-shoulders above any other paper. Even the *New York Times*."

Fat chance on both counts, was my unspoken reaction. And it turned out to be accurate.

Lesley, Alice and I went to lunch at a restaurant not far away that had valet parking and where Mr. Stanford often took his own lunch, we were told. We ordered, and soon Stanford strolled through the door. He came over to our table, bent down, and adjusted the Stanford gold shield pin on Alice's business suit. Then he disappeared into the back of the room where his private table awaited.

3
Allen goes broke, Act 1

Robert Allen Stanford graduated from Baylor University in 1974. Baylor is a Baptist school in Waco, Texas, founded more than 150 years ago by a group of Texans led by Judge R.E.B. Baylor. With an average attendance of about 14,000 students, its leafy campus is among the most beautiful in the nation, comprising dozens of buildings in classic Georgian and Victorian motifs with sumptuous landscaping and gurgling water fountains. This is where Allen Stanford might have developed his architectural predilections. He later claimed, some people say, that he was something of a gridiron hero at the school, a quarterback for the Bears, and although he has the physical look of a field general, no one has been able to find any record of his throwing anything beyond the odd fraternity party.

Although he also claims to have followed in the footsteps of his family's many years of financial management, his grandfather Lodis Stanford was of course just a barber in Mexia and then an insurance agent. Allen and his father James, now operating as Stanford Financial, were able to put together some real-estate deals. They reportedly made some serious money buying up distressed properties in Houston after the 1980s oil crash and selling them off when things recovered. At least this is what Allen claims, although the story has some problems.

As anyone who was around Allen Stanford for any length of time knows, he was fond of saying that it was his brilliant grandfather, Lodis Stanford, who built the rock-ribbed foundations of the Stanford Financial Group some 75 years before. Portraits of the saintly Lodis appeared on the walls of all Stanford offices, peering approvingly down on the empire he reputedly founded. But Lodis Stanford did no such thing. Stanford Financial of Mexia was established not by Lodis but by James. It might be a harmless fiction, but it is fiction nonetheless.

According to an article by *Business Week*'s Matthew Goldstein, within a couple years of his leaving Baylor, Robert Allen went into the fitness industry. Stanford's associates, Goldstein writes, say he opened his first gym in Waco with the new-fangled Nautilus bodybuilding equipment, and then spread to other Texas sites. He called the stores Total Fitness Centers. He was doing fine until he attempted to establish a branch in downtown Houston. The money he was using to get the new enlarged and improved mega-store opened in the city was being supplied from his moderately successful other, smaller Total Fitness Centers. But he had over-reached.

The sudden collapse of the oil market, on which Houston was built, had the city reeling. Offices in the tower he had his Total Fitness Center installed in quickly emptied out, and Stanford was rapidly running short of dough. In 1984, he and his wife Susan filed for bankruptcy. Court records show they had nearly $230,000 in assets and a grinding $13.5 million in liabilities. How this comports with the tale about making a killing off distressed real estate is puzzling.

Anyway, time to reload. Stanford and his wife went off to the Caribbean to lick their wounds and do some scuba-diving. In Aruba, Allen met one Frans Vingerhoedt, a Dutchman living on that Netherlands Antilles island with an idea or two about the offshore-banking business. Stanford and his new pal Vingerhoedt, who remained with Stanford Financial Group until the last dog was shot in 2009, set their sights on the island of Montserrat, a British colony a few miles west of Antigua. The mid-1980s was the time of burgeoning offshore banks all over the Caribbean as the Reagan boom years in America were making lots of people rich and some needed a place to stash their money away from the IRS and the civil, including the divorce, courts. But the real lucre was from South and Central America, largely from drug cartels with the colossal amount of cash that industry was generating. Stanford claims that the money, said to be about $6 million, to open Guardian International Bank in Montserrat came from his father's real estate business in Houston. But this story founders on the fact that the offshore bank was opened a couple of years *after* his father had sold his business, and for an amount nowhere near $6 million. Other accounts say Stanford got the money from Aruban oil workers. Both stories are doubtful.

At any rate, Montserrat was English soil, not an independent country like Antigua just across the water. British authorities took a look at some advertisements Guardian was running in Latin America, chiefly Venezuela, Colombia, Ecuador, Mexico and other bastions of financial rectitude, and didn't like what they saw, especially "guaranteed returns" exceeding 10 percent on certificates of deposit. It didn't smell right.

The Brits told Stanford to knock off the come-ons or leave Montserrat. So he and Vingerhoedt "banged water," as they say in the West Indies, to Antigua, into the arms of the folk hero and nation's leader Vere Cornwall Bird, Sr.

Antigua had become independent of Britain, although still a Commonwealth member, in 1981. To this day parades are held and rousing patriotic speeches are delivered by local orators on November 1, celebrating the long struggle for Antigua's freedom. "What really happen," one old Antiguan told me, "was dat Vere Bird go to London and acks if da island become a free country, like Jamaica and Barbados. And da English say, 'Where do we sign?' "

Vere C. "Papa" Bird was a large man in stature and in the hearts of all Antiguans. With barely a grammar-school education, he was among the fabled labor leaders of the Caribbean that railed against the injustices of the ruling plantocracies. In the folklore of the island, an August 1951 strike against the British planters was instigated by the brash Vere Bird. A big crowd of workers, led by Bird, had gathered near a now-hallowed Tamarind tree at the entrance to the village of Bethesda. The President of the Employers' Association, an Englishman named Moody-Stuart, warned the crowd that everyone was losing money, that 50,000 tons of sugarcane was still standing and needed to be harvested, and that the people would have nothing to eat if the strike went on. Bird held his ground and thundered, "We eat cockles and da widdy-widdy bush. We drink da pon' water." Bird's Antigua Trades and Labour Union dug in (and the sugarcane workers apparently did indeed survive on the weeds and cockles) and the strike lasted until December. There was a harvest that year, but it was well below the average take. Bird's union later formed the Antigua Labour Party, which ruled the island under colonial status and later under independence for decades with Papa Bird at its head.

As was charged by many Antiguans and foreigners alike, the post-colonial Antiguan government was shamelessly corrupt, which did not particularly distinguish it from most other Caribbean nations and colonies: What is graft and corruption to most of the world is standard operating procedure in the Caribbean. Antiguan-born-and-raised writer Jamaica Kincaid (née Elaine Richardson) in her memoir *A Small Place* referred to the island as "a monument to rottenness." Scandals came and went, including gun-running to South Africa and to Colombian drug mobsters, disappearances of foreign-aid money from Kuwait and France, and a notorious incident in which one of Bird's sons, Ivor, was in 1995 arrested at the Antigua airport reportedly carrying 25 pounds of cocaine. He was fined and later took over managing the Bird-family-controlled radio station. And in 1996 American officials charged (correctly) that Russian gangsters had infiltrated the island, running amok with money-laundering, arms-peddling and extortion schemes. While many of these disgraces took place during the time Stanford was developing his Antigua operations, he remained untainted, but it's hard to believe he was in the dark about all the shenanigans going on.

Whether the Guardian International Bank of Montserrat had any substantial funds is questionable. Some place its assets at the time at about $2 million. At any rate, in the late 1980s Stanford was able to shoulder up to the elderly Bird and get assurances that he'd get no grief from the government if he moved his bank to Antigua, which he promptly did, renaming it Stanford International Bank. He then bought the failing local commercial Bank of Antigua for a fire-sale price and Stanford was off and running with the little Caribbean nation firmly tucked under his arm.

To the two existing small branches of the Bank of Antigua, one at the bottom of High Street in the capital, St.

John's, and the other at Nelson's Dockyard in English Harbour on the southern reaches of the island, Stanford added a third branch at the airport, in the parish of Coolidge, a handsome Georgian edifice with lush landscaping and a nursery run by a professional horticulturalist. Antiguans were not sure they liked this carpetbagger from Houston, but with the vigorous compliance of the beatified Papa Bird there wasn't much they could do about it.

While Stanford the offshore banker would later say he wouldn't touch the drug barons with a bargepole, when you open an offshore bank they are certainly going to find you. And, according to some speculation, Stanford could not have gotten started in the absence of suspect funds.

Only once that I know of was Stanford's operation caught taking dirtied money, when in 1997 two Mexican nationals somehow got their ill-gotten gains into SIB in Antigua, allegedly via the Houston office of Stanford Financial Group. As I remember it (I was told by Stanford to do a story on the deal for the *Antigua Sun* that would be an apologia, if not a *mea culpa*, for his bank), a Stanford broker in Houston took deposits of about $3 million on behalf of SIB, and the feds caught onto the deal. Stanford was fined and had to give the money to the feds, the broker was sacked, and when the U.S. authorities demanded that Antigua tighten up its banking laws, Stanford hired a Miami consultant, Tom Cash of Kroll International, a former Drug

Enforcement Agency special agent, to help write new regulations, directed wholly by Stanford. Even the Antigua government had to concede this was opening the henhouse door to the foxes and Stanford was asked to withdraw his services, at least the visible ones. In the end, the new regulations didn't amount to much of a difference, and Antigua continued to be one of the most poorly regulated offshore venues in the world.

Like any entrepreneur, Stanford was a gambler, even though he forbade any of his employees from setting foot in the island's casinos. He knew his game. He knew what face to wear. When Hurricane Luis came roaring through in the fall of 1995, Stanford quickly flew down scores of generators and handed them out to people who had no electricity – which was everyone – until he ran out of the machines. He started up a charity called HERO, although I could never figure out what purpose it served, and made other eleemosynary gestures to persuade Antiguans he was a man of generous and kindly impulses. At the same time, he was rolling dice with enormous stakes, and seemed to be winning. As time went by, Stanford more or less quietly amassed a considerable portfolio of Antigua real estate and his international bank rose far above the other 20 or so offshore institutions on the island, many of which were no more than brass-plate operations with one computer and a lone receptionist. Stanford's banks and his development company and his personal presence were all of big shoulders, highly visible and a rich source of local employment. Scorn him if you will, but he had the greenbacks and you didn't. He was pushy, conceited, despotic and ruthless. But handsome is as handsome does. And he was doing it. *How* he was doing it was always the big question.

4
One very long beach

A couple of days after we returned to California, Lesley and I booked a flight to Antigua. Wheels up early in the morning, Southwest Airlines bounced us through Las Vegas, San Antonio, Dallas, Miami and Puerto Rico, where we boarded an American Eagle flight to the island, landing around midnight. We stepped off the twin-turboprop into warm, damp, fragrant tropical air.

Even though we had travelled throughout much of the world and lived in places like Switzerland and France and England, this arrival on a tiny island in the vast Caribbean Sea had our hearts pumping. We were flush with excitement. Here we were, in our 50s, on the verge of yet another great adventure.

Waiting for us were a balding, rotund, middle-aged man, Bernie Cools-Lartigue, who identified himself as a "the airport manager," and a drop-dead-beautiful young woman, Cynthia Roach, Mr. Stanford's personal assistant, who had milk-chocolate skin and a gently sloping long neck sculpted from an Egyptian frieze. Slight and statuesque, she carried herself with remarkable grace, the kind of woman that makes men shorten their breath and go slightly tongue-tied. This, I thought, is the person Central Casting should have sent over to play Cleopatra. She made Liz Taylor look like a milkmaid. She also had brought along her boyfriend.

After dealing with stern-faced customs and immigration functionaries and biding a rather long time for our luggage to make the hundred-yard trek from the plane to the carousel, Cynthia's boyfriend drove us along pot-hole-studded roads to the Colonna Beach Hotel on a small bay on the north side of the island. As we were checking in, we heard a busy chirping sound wafting into the open-air reception area.

"What's that noise?" Lesley asked Cynthia.

"What noise?"

"The chirping."

"Oh," Cynthia said. "Tree frogs. After you've been here awhile, you hardly notice them."

The water in the little bay sparkled with reflected light and gentle waves flopped on the stony beach. We checked in, and Lesley and I hugged Cynthia, Lesley hugged Bernie and Cynthia's boyfriend and I shook hands exuberantly, much I assume to their surprise, since we had known them for approximately an hour.

The next morning we arose and looked out onto the water: an impossibly blue-green Caribbean inside a reef to our left and a cobalt, white-capped Atlantic Ocean to our right, high wispy clouds in a too-blue sky. Out in the water, a couple of handsome sailboats listed before the wind. *Dear Mom, wish you were here.*

At nine o'clock we collected ourselves in a meeting room at the hotel with a few "Stanford people." There were Bernie and Cynthia, Keva Margetson and Mona Quintyne. Keva was the local Stanford public-relations manager and Mona was the head of human resources for Antigua. They were all disarmingly congenial, terribly smart, perfectly dressed and adorned with the Stanford Eagle pin. None of them, of course, had the foggiest idea about newspaper publishing, and we asked and answered dozens of questions about the job, Antigua, California, Mr. Stanford's businesses, the government, the legal system and where the best beaches were. "Antigua is one very long beach surrounding a tropical island," Keva said.

After the meeting, Mona took us to the police station in Coolidge to buy temporary drivers' licenses. She handed us the keys to a company car, a little white Toyota, and a map of Antigua.

"Wander around the island and take it in," Mona said. "Don't worry. You can't get lost for long."

We drove into the capital town, St. John's, an unassuming sprawl of storefronts, offices, banks, restaurants, tiny casinos, street vendors and bustle. The sidewalks were fairly treacherous, set willy-nilly with startling changes in altitude. The town sloped down from the Antigua Recreation Ground and Independence Drive to Heritage Quay, where a monster cruise ship was disgorging pale-faced throngs. There was no place to park, and the pedestrians were outpacing the beeping, creeping cars. Down near the water scores of open-air shops hawked T-shirts and tacky souvenirs, and air-conditioned shops were selling duty-free cigarettes and liquor and jewelry and locally created clothing in bold West Indian colors and soft pastels. We at last found a lucky place to ditch the car a few blocks from where we had a first-rate Chinese lunch at a closet-sized restaurant called Delightful.

We then set off, heading south out of town, passing through the edges of St. John's where diminutive, scruffy houses stood cheek by jowl, looking poor and third-worldish, but without squalor or sadness. In the West Indies, we were to learn, poverty is what most people live with, yet it does little to blunt their cheer or pride. With rare exception, Antiguans are generous and warm, with not much to lose and seldom given to grousing about their simple lives. They are often shy, save for a few ignorant and misled young men, and always quick to laugh.

Emerging from the outskirts of St. John's, the road flowed into a wide expanse of green pastures, with small herds of goats in solemn rumination. In the distance, low, verdant hills rose into a sky flecked with gauzy clouds. A string of little villages came and went along the narrow carriageway – Ebenezer, Jennings, Bolans, where on the side of the road a skinned carcass of beef had been hung on a tree, its butcher carving off gobbets for sale. No refrigeration, just swarms of flies and eager customers, women in long cotton dresses and kerchiefs on their heads. Tiny dwellings perching on six columns of four or five concrete blocks were scattered here and there. These were chattel houses, small enough to be moved on donkey carts, architecture left over from plantation days when their occupants could travel with the harvest of sugarcane from farm to farm.

Past Bolans, the road rose abruptly then fell into another valley and the pavement gave way to a bumpy, coral-strewn stretch down to Darkwood Beach, where it swung eastward, rose again, fell again, with mangrove and cassie bush on the seaside and softly sloping foothills on the left, where thousands of acres of sugarcane once grew in the fertile, sun-soaked soil. The village of Old Road came into view, the oldest settlement in Antigua, dating back to around 1630. Horses, ponies, goats, cows, donkeys and barefoot children roamed unfettered across the wide upland. In the sea to the south, a smudge near the horizon was the French island of Guadeloupe. And in the distance to the west, you could see Montserrat and its smoldering volcano Soufriére.

We squeezed through the eastern edge of Old Road, with its little houses tightly packed on both sides pinching the way, and began the climb into the rain forest on Fig Tree Drive, named not for figs but after what everyone but Antiguans calls bananas. The fruit grew in smallish gardens on the lower reaches of the drive, which was twisty and narrow, hung with ropy vines and shaded with ferns. As we rose into the forest, we passed by thick, mossy ancient trees standing in the soggy, cool air, while narrow creeks flowed through concrete swales across the road.

Fig Tree Drive ultimately spilled out onto All Saints Road, running from St. John's in the north down to English Harbour and Falmouth Harbour in the south. At the intersection was a Catholic church, set back from the opposite side of the road on a low hill. Our Lady of Perpetual Help, painted the color of California Zinfandel, was erected in the 1930s. It was, I thought, one of the prettiest churches I'd ever seen. We were in the village of Tyrells, about halfway between the capital town and the southern bays.

A few miles along we came to a high spot where English and Falmouth Harbours swam into view, gorgeous bays bristling with sailboat masts and lined with massive private yachts, all blinding white and oozing extravagance.

English Harbour, one of the safest hurricane holes in the Antilles, is guarded from the east by Shirley Heights. We went up to take a look.

Along the way was a rank of ruined buildings, the former Shirley Heights Military Complex, built in the 1780s to train and house local troops and officers under the command of Governor Sir Thomas Shirley. At the top was a small restaurant near a cliff, where we took tea (Lesley is hopelessly English) and Coca-Cola and looked down on the two harbors hundreds of feet below. We had our first flying-fish sandwich.

Shirley Heights to me seemed like a power spot, a place where you feel charged with an enlivened psyche, the rush you get at Big Sur or Mount Fuji or the Grand Canyon. In the years to come, Lesley and I would escape to Shirley Heights often, when the stress of work needed relief or to show visiting friends what they were missing.

We got back to the hotel as the sun was setting. Down near the swimming pool ("the largest in the Caribbean"), a clutch of people stood looking intently out to sea. I asked a woman what the attraction was.

"Green flash," she said.

"I'm sorry?"

"On really clear days like this," a man standing nearby explained, "just as the last pinpoint of sunlight clears the horizon, a flash of green sometimes comes off the water. Watch."

And suddenly, there it was. A burst of bright iridescent emerald, lasting maybe half a second.

"Pretty damn amazing, eh?" the green-flash expert said.

"What the hell causes that?" I asked.

"Nobody really knows," he said, shrugging.

At dinner, over broiled langouste and deep-fried *fruits de mer*, we talked about our first day in Antigua.

"You know," I said. "It's funny that Stanford wanted us to come down here to see if we thought we could live in Antigua. Right about now, I can't imagine why anyone would want to live somewhere else."

To which we drank.

5
End of an affair

When R. Allen Stanford's world collapsed in 2009, it was clear to me that whether he was, as the Securities and Exchange Commission charged, running a "massive ongoing fraud" or not, he was no longer, apparently, a billionaire or a millionaire or even a thousandaire. At least he could not access whatever money he did have, since all his assets had been frozen by the SEC. But he had lost, guilty or not, his most critical asset. The one overarching, *ne plus ultra,* characteristic of anyone who manages other people's money is the ability to inspire trust. As far as Stanford's financial edifice was concerned, that trust had been sucked out in a heartbeat. And even if the SEC used extremely heavy-handed tactics in going after Stanford (chiefly because it was smarting from its utter failure to detect the Bernie Madoff scandal), even a sniff of something awry will send investors to the exits as from a theater on fire.

People whom I talked to after The Crash, people who worked for Stanford, told me they could see the end coming many months before the ax came down. Yet even casual observers of Stanford's behavior in the run-up to the downfall could have predicted it. I, for one, thought I saw it coming and told friends and even some Virgin Islands political figures to keep at arm's length from the man. They dismissed my warnings as the grumbling of a bitter disgruntled former employee who had ulterior personal motives. Far from disgruntled, I was in fact deeply grateful that I got out from under the Stanford tyranny before I had invested my future in a guy I suspected, from day one, was not what he pretended to be.

The signs were clear as early as 2004, when the United Progressive Party of Antigua (which is really a coalition of various groups aligned against the formerly eternal rule of the Bird family's Antigua Labour Party) swept Prime Minister Lester Bird (V.C. Bird's son) and the ALP from office, winning 12 of the 17 seats in the House of Representatives. The new prime minister, Baldwin Spencer, had been opposed to the ALP's embrace of Stanford for all the years Allen and his companies had free rein in the tiny country. After that election, it appears that Stanford opened talks with the government of St. Kitts/Nevis, another former British colony 60 miles west of Antigua. Stanford began publishing a sort of sister paper to the *Antigua Sun* on the two-island nation, the *St. Kitts Sun*. But something must have turned sour there, like perhaps the St. Kitts government's concerns it might become the next Stanford-owned island. What unraveled any agreements I don't know; most of Stanford's business dealings are *sub rosa*. What *was* apparent was that Stanford was not enamored of the new Antigua government, and the feeling was mutual.

The other newspaper in Antigua, the *Daily Observer*, had never let an opportunity to bash Stanford go by, and was (is) closely aligned with the UPP. Stanford knew he no longer had the top officials on the island in his pocket, and he was casting about for some place to move, ever so gradually, his Caribbean headquarters to.

By that time, of course, much of the ALP's coddling of Stanford had made him the largest private landowner in Antigua. Along with his other holdings, he had bought a small islet just off the northern coast, Maiden Island, where he planned to build for himself a palace and become the island's only resident. When he brought in heavy machinery to start construction, parts of the reef suffered serious damage, sparking howls from environmental groups and UPP ministers. The plan was later abandoned and Stanford promised to repair some of the injuries to the reef, and then proclaimed that the island would become a venue for ecological research. But everyone could see that the Antigua game had fundamentally changed for Sir Allen.

In 2007, a close friend of mine, a St. Croix real-estate broker, told me over coffee one morning that he had just closed a $9.3 million deal for the sale of the Henry J. Kaiser estate on Recovery Hill overlooking Christiansted.

"Who bought it?" I asked.

"A guy named Stanford."

Slightly stunned, I said, "Don't tell me the rest of his name is R. Allen ..."

"Yeah," he said. "You know him?"

By then I had lived on St. Croix for almost eight years. After leaving the *Antigua Sun*, I went to work in Trinidad for the Associated Press and in late 1998 I was offered the job as editor at the *St. Croix Avis*, a paper that had been published without interruption since 1844. After two years at the *Avis* (Lesley also worked there as assistant managing editor) I retired and went back to freelancing and book-writing. Even so, I couldn't resist the opportunity to become news director of a local radio station, Paradise 93.5 FM, where I broadcast the news daily for about a year. Then I re-retired. The report that my old pal R. Allen Stanford had arrived in "my" town, guns blazing, came as a bit of a shock.

But this, to me, was even more evidence that Stanford's affair with Antigua was maybe on the rocks. Or something.

Word spread quickly that a Texas billionaire was moving to St. Croix, a mogul who had a reputation of spending big and thinking big and hiring big. With St. Croix's chronic underemployment and somewhat backward economy, this was music to everyone's ears. He demonstrated his customary flamboyance by calling a press conference to break ground on a multi-million-dollar project at the airport, announcing, "St. Croix is my home now." (A quote from years before in Antigua: "This is my home now.") The governor, various local senators, chamber-of-commerce types and select Stanford People all beamed for the cameras. This was to be Stanford's "headquarters for all my Caribbean operations." Goodbye Antigua? Hello St. Croix? It sure looked that way.

A few of my friends who knew I had once worked for Stanford and who were hankering to get jobs with him asked me what I thought. Trying my best not to look bitter and disgruntled, I usually said something like, "He pays well and benefits are good. But if you take a job with him, sooner or later – *sooner or later* – you'll regret it." Lesley and I were the only people in St. Croix who rolled our eyes and shook our heads when the subject of Stanford came up. Because we knew, or thought we knew, that Stanford would one day auger in and burn, taking everyone else with him in a spectacular finale.

In rapid-fire succession, Stanford began forking out millions as the locals swooned. Nearly $10 million for the Kaiser estate, $7 million for a mansion formerly owned by pianist/comedian Victor Borge and now having been converted to an office complex by another shifty Crucian resident, Jeffrey Prosser, who had gone bankrupt after amassing a fortune on the island and living it up in Palm Beach and other tony spots, spending, like Stanford, other people's money. Sir Allen then bought a decrepit hotel on the Christiansted Boardwalk and started to tear it down. Then a commercial building on King Street and another near the water on Strand Street. "He paid too much for all these properties," one real-estate broker observed. "He was getting lots of lousy advice." I can't say who he was getting the advice from, but I did notice that Frans Vingerhoedt was still in tow.

To Lesley and me, this was all *déjà vu*. We had seen Stanford spend lavishly on Antigua real estate, on ambitious and often impossible schemes that were intended to make him look brilliant and prescient, a Master of the Universe. But there is a bottom to every barrel. Stanford, while telling his investors their money was going into publicly traded equities, bonds, precious metals and other highly liquid assets, was in fact, according to the SEC and anyone else with his eyes open, buying overpriced real estate and stakes in private-equity companies, both highly illiquid, and other questionable business ploys. His personal life-style was kingly. We joked that he would love to buy and move into Versailles whenever it goes up for sale. And maybe even rebuild it in his own "vision."

We had seen first-hand his modus operandi in Antigua, and that included starting up the *Antigua Sun*, among many, many even more imprudent investments, a few of the most mind-numbing ones we'll look into later in this book. But in Antigua it was the *Sun* that we were responsible for, to create the paper and make it profitable, the latter being made more and more difficult by Allen Stanford.

A month or so after we had made our first visit to Antigua, having closed our failing newspaper, packing our household furnishings into a shipping container and saying tearful goodbyes to our friends in California, we arrived once again on the island, in December of 1996, to embark on the project. In our first meeting with Stanford, I told him he should expect the new paper to lose money for at least two years, maybe three, which even under the best of circumstances is normal for most small businesses. He indicated (in a haughty rejoinder) that he knew all about starting up new ventures and I should just worry about making the paper "head and shoulders" above every other local paper in the universe. Indeed, he had visions of distributing the *Sun* throughout the Caribbean, which told me he hadn't a clue about the newspaper business. And that was fine with me, since I didn't want anyone second-guessing my know-how or my methods. That was perhaps strike one, since by the time we were up and running Stanford phoned me every day, commented on every issue of the paper, and demanded, as with all his other companies, we submit weekly reports by e-mail to him in Houston or wherever he happened to be.

But the circumstances were *not* the best. They were not even good. Stanford's intentions were to counter the political influence of the two then-existing papers on the island, the *Daily Observer* and *The Outlet,* the latter being published by a Marxist intellectual named Tim Hector. *The*

Outlet was an awful rag, full of articles that had been photocopied and reprinted from the *New York Times* or *Washington Post*, without permission or attribution, and the Bolshevik ravings of Hector in his weekly column "Fan the Flames." The *Observer* was (still is) an 8.5 x 11-inch pamphlet whose main mission was to berate and attack the Bird political machine. To publish a better paper than these two was child's play, but the highly charged politics of Antigua would put up a formidable obstacle to a new newspaper's chances of even modest success.

If your car was painted red, the official color of the Antigua Labour Party, or if you happened to wear a red shirt or blouse in public, that meant that you were a Bird supporter. If your car was blue, you were for the United Progressive Party. I made the error of buying a bright-red Toyota pickup truck, and my loyalties were revealed. I soon realized why every car and truck that Stanford owned on the island was white. When I wanted to buy a van to distribute the *Sun*, Stanford said, "OK. But make sure it's white."

In this sort of atmosphere, nearly everything was interpreted as a political gesture. If a local merchant were to advertise in the *Sun*, he was automatically supporting Stanford and by extension Lester Bird. This attitude, I learned early on, was all but insuperable. Ads from car dealers, department stores, real-estate agents, professionals, grocers – even classifieds – were nearly impossible to land. UPP supporters laughed our sales people out the door; ALP supporters apologized, but said they really couldn't take the risk of losing customers by advertising in a Stanford/Bird paper. And this is not special pleading: The other two papers had similar problems. If you bought space in the *Daily Observer* or *Outlet,* you were against Bird and the ALP. The *Observer* survived mainly on its circulation. *The Outlet* never made a dime. It slowly became clear to me that the *Antigua Sun* would never be profitable unless it could command a readership of at least 5,000 newsstand-sales copies a day. (Most newspapers strive to capture a market penetration of 10 percent of the population, which in the case of the *Sun* would be about 6,500 copies.) Otherwise, it would prevail exclusively through the largesse of Stanford. And at the beginning the *Sun* was just a weekly, then later a twice-weekly as we moved toward daily publication. A non-daily didn't have a chance. The only advertising we could drum up were what are called "national accounts," for products that are sold more-or-less worldwide. No one could accuse Huggies of political bias. So I spent quite a bit of time in Trinidad, where most of the advertising agencies for national brands were headquartered. But it was never enough.

On top of that paralyzing situation was Stanford's demands for excellence. Although the ad agency that created our logo (and it was a beauty) was an in-house Stanford division in Houston, we were charged $5,000. The

Sun had to pay $16,000 for our move from California. We were billed tens of thousands for work preparing our offices in the Woods Centre near St. John's by Stanford Development Company. We had to buy all our office furniture, equipment, fixtures, computers and supplies through Houston as well. The cost was two or three times what it would have been had we equipped the offices from local sources.

The point being: I was not running the *Antigua Sun* even though my title was Editor and General Manager. R. Allen Stanford was running the *Antigua Sun*. By the time we published our first issue in April of 1997, we were deep in a financial hole on the books and getting regular injections of cash from Stanford, or rather Stanford International Bank and Stanford Financial Group.

Our newsroom was home to the best reporters and writers in Antigua. Our sales manager was a well-known and much-admired young woman born and raised on the island. Our computer system ran flawlessly (thanks to Laurence Arevalo). Our graphics and layout people were gifted professionals, one of whom I brought down from California.

There were only a couple of problems, really: No advertising and a feeble circulation, without which we were spinning our wheels. When I spoke of my frustrations and fears to Stanford, which I did on two or three occasions, he said, "I don't care about that."

And I really wasn't the editor either, in the sense I had real editorial control. Stanford himself assigned many stories, or at least subjects to pursue, and if we printed something that displeased him, he was never at pains to let me know about it. And despite his stated indifference to our parlous finances, one day Stanford burst into the *Sun's* offices and called the entire staff into the newsroom (on a day I was in Trinidad, hat in hand at some ad agency). He then went on to upbraid reporters, copy editors, film strippers, pagination staff and the receptionist. He brought with him a young woman from SIB, which confused the staff until he summoned her in. She gave him a bag, and from it he withdrew thousands of Eastern Caribbean dollars and threw them on the floor of the newsroom.

"That's how much money I am losing every day with this paper. Twenty thousand dollars," he bellowed. "And you are going to change that or I'll get people who will."

Maria Brooks, our irrepressible British-Antiguan production manager, asked, "Are you going to leave that money here, Mr. Stanford?" Shortly afterwards, she found work elsewhere.

No one in the room had anything whatsoever to do with the profits or losses of the newspaper except Stanford himself. It was like a bus driver who had run off the road berating his passengers on their poor driving skills. It was, I thought when I heard about the incident, a good thing I was in Trinidad that day. That saved me from saying, "Maybe things will improve if you let *me* be the editor and general manager and you stay the hell out of it."

That would have been *my* last day.

In the summer of 2008, after Stanford had made his belly-flop entrance into St. Croix the year before, the writing started appearing on the wall. He announced he was "rethinking" his harebrained Twenty20 cricket fiasco. Construction on his Caribbean Financial Headquarters and fixed-base aviation operation at the airport came to an abrupt halt with only a little sod having been turned.

Late in 2008, on the local grapevine, rumors of mysterious meetings of Stanford executives were circulating. And the Kaiser mansion – with its two swimming pools, out buildings and the mansion itself – had been flattened by bulldozers to make way for ... Versailles? But work had stopped. On Recovery Hill you could hear a pin drop.

And in February of 2009 the Stanford Eagle came plummeting to earth. His offices were shuttered. His 120-foot Sea Eagle yacht was taken to St. Thomas by a local receiver for safe-keeping, and some 80 dumbfounded Stanford workers, now unemployed and unpaid, trickled away with hanging heads and broken hearts.

6
Pirates of the Caribbean

Most of the nations and colonies of the Lesser Antilles are either in permanent economic crisis or teetering on the brink. There are exceptions, but they are few. Trinidad, despite its ugly and often violent political animosities, is awash in oil and natural gas. It doesn't need, and doesn't get, many tourists. Barbados, as the saying goes, is a British Isle with palm trees, having retained much of its English culture. It held off Cromwell's Roundheads in the 17th century and has been staunchly royalist ever since, with fairly sturdy governments and usually responsible labor leaders. The Cayman Islands, a British colony, has the fifth largest banking venue in the world, with nearly 300 offshore financial institutions as well as one of the biggest hedge-fund industries on earth. Cayman Islanders have an annual per-capita income of more than $42,000, the highest by far in the Eastern Caribbean. (Compare Antigua's PCI: about $14,000.)

Even so, about 70 percent of the Cayman Islands' GDP is tourism-related. And this is the rub: Tourism is what keeps the Lesser Antilles afloat. Without it, nearly every island in the archipelago would go into financial meltdown. Tourism is the largest industry by revenue in the world. It is fiercely competitive and its clients are fickle. *"Where to this year, Honey? Paris? Bali? Disney World?"* And few industries are as vulnerable to economic downturns as tourism. Every dime spent by tourists is "disposable income," so when things get tight, there's little to dispose of. With an average tourism dependency of around 65 percent of GDP throughout the Lesser Antilles, nearly every island-nation or colony (or other political situations, like the French *départements* of Guadeloupe and Martinique or the complicated Dutch Antilles arrangements with the Netherlands) fights for its life by attracting every visitor it can get. On top of this, almost all the tourism infrastructure is controlled by overseas companies, who own and operate the hotels, the casinos, the cruise ships, the airlines and the retail restaurant and merchandise chains. Even the smaller tourism-related businesses, like dive shops, sightseeing boats, parasailing and the like, are often run by Americans or Europeans, not local blacks descended largely from the slaves who worked the sugar, cotton and tobacco plantations from the 17th through the middle of the 19th centuries. The retail industries – car dealerships and department stores, for example – in most of the islands are owned not by blacks but by Middle Easterners (Arabs from Syria, Palestine and Lebanon, mostly), whose families might have arrived generations before.

The tourism industry in the Lesser Antilles burgeoned over the years following World War II, providing a trickle-down income for the black majorities, but still left most families in *de facto* poverty or near to it. Unlike developed nations, the middle classes of the Caribbean were insignificant, and mostly restricted to tradesmen and service providers. The cultural imperatives of the people of the Lesser Antilles were an important obstacle: The blacks were, and are, generally lacking in the resources to start businesses, and even if capital was available they are typically not inclined toward entrepreneurship. I am neither a sociologist nor a psychologist, thus I am unqualified to analyze the underlying reasons for such attitudes. But I certainly have seen this reluctance of the majority populations of the islands to embark on risk-taking ventures on many of the islands I have lived on or visited.

Caribbean governments have confronted this dilemma in, one supposes, the only way they could. They created a bloated public sector, providing jobs with generous benefits and pensions, based on labor-movement ideas of fairness and security for the workers. While this strategy did establish a more viable middle class in most cases, it also placed heavy burdens on the governments themselves. It has further led to rampant patronage and, inevitably, widespread corruption. The power to parcel out jobs and largesse creates a concomitant power over people's lives and a compliant constituency at the ballot boxes. No news to the non-socialists among us, but an insidious and virtually irreversible political state of affairs attends all such schemes, and in the long run the cure becomes the disease.

Thus the governments of the Caribbean islands became low-hanging fruit for the promoters and developers and tax avoiders. Bribery and shady deals were and are the way much business is done in the region, and Antigua was a shining example. R. Allen Stanford was not the only capitalist who knew that he could buy island governments as easily as a hot dog at the ball park. A little green grease could open doors, secure permits and get special exceptions to rules. Payoffs masquerading as campaign contributions work wonders and ensure the cooperation of the authorities. That makes doing business a lot easier and far more profitable for those entities seeking favors and permissions.

As with Stanford, the case is made, with good reason, that outside investments accrue many benefits to the little folks who vote, and even though the people know full well where the Minister of Public Works got the money for a new house or car or girlfriend, things are supposed to get better for everyone else as well.

V.S. Naipaul, the Nobel Laureate, once observed that among the black or East Indian populations of the Caribbean it didn't matter if their leaders were crooks or philanderers or deceivers. They were still "one of us." For that remark, he was accused of racism (even though

Naipaul is of East Indian descent). But few would argue he wasn't onto something.

Caribbean leaders, then, do not have much fear about bedding down with rich interlopers and accepting their emoluments, or "campaign contributions." Lester Bird's ALP got turned away in 2004 because the opposition had persuaded enough voters that the Bird dynasty had been giving away the farm, mainly to Stanford, for years. Corruption was not the issue. Handing the nation's real estate, the people's patrimony, away to a Texas high-roller who flew around in private jets and wore $500 shirts was the real issue. One of the slogans the UPP circulated on the run-up to the 2009 election was, "Uncle Stan Wants Your Land," on a poster imitating the famous "Uncle Sam Wants You" recruiting pitch.

All the jobs and the elegant buildings Stanford produced were fine, but the tipping point of dissatisfaction with Stanford's relentless acquisition was nearing and Baldwin Spencer's UPP simply gave it a shove.

No one – almost no one – in Antigua was happy about Stanford's demise. About 800 people worked for one or other of Stanford's companies on the island. But while Antiguans were saying it was "too bad" what happened, they would have preferred that to the anointment of a new King of the Realm. They already had a Queen anyway. Lester Bird, by the way, was returned to office as the minority leader in the 2009 election, and the UPP margin in the House was cut from 12 to 9, out of 17. Bird beat a local attorney, Dr. Errol Cort, who had defected from the ALP to the UPP five years before. When the Bank of Antigua was hammered by its depositors in the Stanford crisis, which exploded just weeks before the 2009 general election, it was Cort as the Minister of Finance who led the effort to shore the bank up and protect people's money. And in an example of how convoluted Caribbean politics can be, Cort was for years the main local lawyer for Stanford, and even though he was now a UPP representative, he was getting a $25,000 retainer every month from Sir Allen, according to newspaper ads run by the ALP before the 2009 election.

The devastation in Antigua from the sudden loss of 800 jobs was an economic train wreck. Most of those who lost their jobs were native Antiguans.

Yet Stanford had managed to buy over time, normally at bargain-basement – "peppercorn" – prices, nearly 1,700 acres of Antigua real estate. After the SEC made its accusations, the Antigua government moved with uncharacteristic alacrity to seize his Bank of Antigua (to staunch the run) and all his holdings. The official explanation of the ruling party was they feared the SEC might grab the land as Stanford's private property, which it technically was. That would mean that the second largest landowner on the island after the Antigua government would be the United States of America. As receivers, the SEC could sell the land to anyone it wanted to; Antigua would have nothing to say about it. The property grab will be opposed by the SEC, and the Antiguans will dig in their heels, and the case will drag on for centuries.

But slinky tax dodgers and rapacious capitalists aren't the only types coddled by the government. Antigua is home to a substantial number of Internet-gambling servers, many residing on the upper floor of the Woods Centre in St. John's. There are no signs indicating who is in the offices, just numbers on each door. The venetian blinds are fully shut, and all you can hear is the low whirr of the electronic looting of the world's stay-at-home poker players. Since the U.S. has laws, however dubious, against gaming on your own computer, Washington has voiced its displeasure at Antigua's *laissez-faire* Internet gambling industry.

In a dispute lasting several years, the World Trade Organization upheld Antigua's complaint that the U.S. was sticking its nose into other people's business. Each offshore gaming operation in Antigua has to pay something like $100,000 every year for a license, but is otherwise free to do what it wants.

The operators themselves are making heaps of money and spending lots of it in Antigua. The bluenose Americans, they said, could go directly to hell. And, in my view, they were exactly right to say so. If fools wanted to give their money to anonymous computer programmers in an anonymous country, that was their mistake, not Antigua's.

The island was also a magnet for hucksters. One day when I was with the paper, a character named Augie Delgado landed in Antigua. Speaking in New Age abstractions and splashing about on the TV and in the papers, Augie had "after 13 long years of hard study," discovered the way to make everyone in Antigua rich, quickly. He called it "empowerment." Delgado characterized his scheme as a "multi-level marketing system" that used a mathematical formula authored by an Italian monk in the 13th century known as the Fibonacci Series. Delgado's "firm" was called Fortuna Alliance, which was a pyramid scam turned on its head, but it was still a pyramid scam.

The *Sun* ran a story covering Delgado at a grip-and-grin event giving a check to a local charity, showing his soft heart and caring ways, the coin of con artists the world over. I took one look at the photograph and said to our investigative reporter Louis Daniel, "This guy's a crook. Let's see what we can find about out him."

Daniel didn't have to look far. The feds, this time the Federal Trade Commission, had raided Delgado's Fortuna Alliance digs in Bellingham, Washington, in March of 1996, claiming the "New Age businessman" had bilked his followers out of as much as $15 million in what appeared to be a complicated pyramid game. At least $5 million of the take had been deposited in the Swiss American Bank of ... Antigua. And that's where Delgado was while the feds were trying to sort out the mess in Bellingham and other American cities.

We ran the story. Delgado was furious. His lawyer called me and threatened a libel suit. Then Stanford phoned. "Are you sure this stuff is true?"

"Yes. Are you worried about a lawsuit?"

"No. We don't worry about lawsuits. We have too many layers. No one could ever get through them."

The next day Delgado's lawyer called again.

"Just wanted to let you know we no longer represent Mr. Delgado or Fortuna Alliance."

Delgado eventually settled with the feds via a consent decree, putting him out of any further monkey business in the U.S. A few weeks after we broke our story, Delgado went somewhere, perhaps Suriname or maybe where Portuguese is spoken in South America, but he wasn't in Antigua any more.

The offshore Swiss American Bank of Antigua, incidentally, itself was embroiled in charges of money laundering a few years later by the United States Senate, which warned a couple of New York City banks against dealing with it and its infamous globe-trotting wheeler-dealer and Israel-born owner, Bruce Rappaport. According to the Consortium for Independent Journalism, Rappaport had shadowy ties to the Reagan administration. "These included: the Iran-contra affair; an Israeli bribery case that involved a U.S.-backed oil pipeline in Iraq; the scandal over the Bank of Credit and Commerce International; a curious shipment of weapons through a melon farm in Antigua to Colombian cocaine kingpins; and the October Surprise mystery [and] the allegations that the 1980 Reagan campaign sabotaged Carter's negotiations to free 52 American hostages held in Iran," as the CIJ reported on its Web site.

And this brings us to the tale of yet another deal-maker banging water to Antigua, Dato Tan Kay Hock.

7
Island in the sun

Tan Sri Dato Tan Kay Hock and his wife, with the splendid name of Puan Sri Datin Tan Swee Bee, are the chief shareholders of the Malaysian corporation Johan Holdings Berhad. Tan Sri is an honorific title conferred by the Malaysian government, and Dato is conferred by any hereditary Sultan ruler of a Malaysian state. The wife is a Puan Sri Datin.

A lawyer by training (in the U.K.), Tan is a very wealthy man. He made a bundle in the public-utility business in Malaysia in his younger years. Today, Johan Holdings has interests in hotels, engineering firms, health foods, Diners Club franchises in Malaysia and Singapore, manufacturing and real estate. In 1996, the Overseas Chinese tycoon showed up in Antigua with a grand plan: He was prepared to purchase Guiana Island and turn it in to a themed "Asian Village" resort. He was going to spend about $600 million on the project, he said. This had Lester Bird's attention briefly diverted from his Texan benefactor R. Allen Stanford.

Guiana Island, snuggled up against the northeastern corner of the island and protected by Crabbs Peninsula on the west and Coconut Hall and a smaller island on the south, curves like an arthritic finger up into the Atlantic Ocean. Its 1,400 or so acres comprise an island that is flat, long and hardly touched by man.

Since the 1960s, the only human residents of the island were Taffy and Bonnie Bufton, an elderly Welsh couple who lived in a ramshackle cottage with no running water or electricity. Their residency was part of the sales agreement when the island was sold to local attorney John Fuller decades ago, whose Guiana Island Farms Limited also owned a few other islands nearby. The agreement provided that the Buftons would retain two acres of land and the house and become technically employed by Fuller as the island's caretakers. They paid no rent.

Guiana Island is home to the rare endangered West Indian whistling duck, the even rarer Antiguan racer snake, some fallow deer, and plenty of mangroves. The Buftons lived there with their few goats, chickens and a little vegetable garden. To reach the mainland they navigated a rude wooden raft across a few hundred feet of water. To call the Buftons eccentric would be understating things. Taffy always seemed to have shaved several days before you ran into him, and Bonnie was as rare a sight as the whistling duck.

From time to time Taffy would raft across the narrow channel, hail a passing public bus, and ride into St. John's. He would sometimes stop by the offices of the *Antigua Sun*, dressed in sweat-moistened cotton shirt, baggy, soiled trousers and tattered leather sandals. He exuded the odor of someone who lived with no running water, but no one gagged. He was, after a fashion, quite lovable. He would rage in imprecation of the government, urge us to expose the injustices and insufferable behavior of Lester Bird and all his criminal henchmen, flirt with the receptionist and the female reporters, and soon disappear as abruptly as he had arrived. Taffy held that Guiana Island was his and Bonnie's, and the Antigua government had better keep its hands off. Indeed, Taffy often proclaimed that he and Bonnie owned the *entire* island by virtue of squatters' rights, which was pure fantasy, but in Taffy's mind there were ample fantasies at large.

"When we were kids," Eli Fuller, the son of John Fuller and the operator of the ecological-tour service Antigua Adventures told me, "we would try to go over to Guiana Island to check it out and Taffy would always chase us off with a shotgun." As it would turn out, Taffy and his guns would get him in big trouble in 1997.

Nonetheless, Lester Bird was charmed by Dato Tan Kay Hock's visions of an Asian Village on Guiana Island and on the nearby mainland next to the village of Parham. Here the Malaysian was to build 250 Asian-style rental units, a water park, hundreds of private residences, a golf course, restaurants selling sushi and Peking duck and dim sum, a full-on casino and a conference center. His clientele would be mostly from Japan, Malaysia, China, Indonesia, Singapore and Taiwan. And he would fly them in from Asia on his own Airbus airliners.

To bolster his bona fides, Tan brought in a team of architects, public-relations flacks, engineers and money-handlers. At a hotel on Dickenson Bay he held court, displaying elaborate and impressive artists' renderings of the coming Asian Village and fielding questions from the press. A tiny, soft-spoken man, Tan seemed an unlikely business mogul, but when I set my reporters on his trail, everything seemed indisputable. He was rich, powerful and persuasive. Stanford loved him, perhaps seeing in Tan an Asian version of a hard-driving American entrepreneur.

But here was my question: Why would folks from Southeast Asia want to fly 7,000 miles to stay in a place that looked exactly like Southeast Asia? I conveyed my doubts to Stanford.

"Look, Bob," he said. "The guy's going to spend $600 million developing the project. Lots of jobs for Antiguans. Lots of tourists from Asia. You don't understand how these things work."

I guess not. But neither did Taffy and Bonnie Bufton. After Bird agreed to sell Tan the island and about 80 acres of land outside of Parham for $6 million, a peppercorn price if there ever was one, the only obstacle was the old Welsh couple, who had no intention of selling anything. Bird offered the Buftons nearly $200,000 to clear out, along with a new house on the mainland and maybe a nice car. Taffy gave Bird the bird. No one who knew the Buftons was surprised. Taffy and Bonnie lived the kind of life that impossible dreamers the world over would envy. No neighbors, no debts, no noise, no job, no insinuating civilization to deal with. Just the goats and the chickens, rainwater to drink and friendly fallow deer and whistling ducks and tree frogs chirping through the sultry tropical nights. And if anyone tried to bother them, out came the shotgun.

As the Dato Tan Kay Hock saga played out, our investigations revealed that Tan might have been dealing with the Bird regime since at least as early as 1995. It was in that year that the government was looking into acquiring Guiana Island from John Fuller via "compulsory purchase," or eminent domain. If Stanford was aware of the master scheme, he never let on to me. And he must certainly have known, since he was an intimate of Lester Bird and the prime minister relied on Stanford for financial counsel, which might not always have been objective.

In August of 1997, the government finally took the land from Fuller for the condemnation price of $10 million. The Buftons were ordered to clear out.

In December of 1997, Taffy Bufton stormed into the law office of Vere Bird, Jr., got into a shouting match and brandished a revolver. In the struggle, Taffy shot Bird in the jaw before being subdued. Vere Bird survived, which was probably not Taffy's intention. The next day the police physically removed Bonnie Bufton from Guiana Island. Taffy was in jail on an attempted-murder charge. To no one's surprise, the charges were later dropped. Taffy was released, and died a few years later. Bonnie, who ultimately was paid about $375,000 in damages for the government's forcible and quite illegal removal from her land and in compensation for the couple's loss of their home and improbable lifestyle, still lives in Antigua and drives a Jeep.

The deal with Dato Tan was signed. His company would put up an initial $1 million and made detailed promises as to what the project would entail, when it was to be completed and when the rest of the money would be paid. A ground-breaking ceremony was thrown on a bulldozed meadow across the channel from Guiana Island. Three days later, Tan shelled out the first $1 million payment. That was essentially the last time Tan's company went anywhere near the place. Construction never really started in earnest. The government and Tan's lawyers exchanged heated letters; the Bird administration demanded action, but Tan asked for extension after extension, citing the severe Asian economic downturn in 1998. His financing for the $600 million scheme had dried up, he said. Stanford waited on the sidelines.

Note that what Dato Tan Kay Hock paid for Guiana Island was less than 60 percent of what the government was to pay Fuller in its taking. This is entirely typical of how power-hitters take advantage of Caribbean governments: Come down with an ambitious plan, show them the money, and get enormous concessions on the promise of jobs and economic development. Get the land cheap. Renege on the deal. Sell the land as a "work in progress." Take the cash and chuckle at the naïveté of the benighted West Indians. Stanford strayed from the pattern in that he actually put up buildings and did more or less what he said he would. But he was still getting acreage (like the airport complex) on the cheap. And that's how the game is played. It's the Shark Strategy: Eat the weak and the wounded.

The ball was batted from court to court over the next few years. Tan's lawyers said he was not in violation of the development contract; the Bird administration said he was, and threatened to quash the deal altogether. They had yet to pay either John Fuller's company for the compulsory sale of Guiana Island or the Bufton claims. And that's where matters stood when the UPP assumed control of the government in March of 2004. On August 18 of that year, Attorney General Justin Simon addressed the country, describing what had transpired with the Asian Village project, essentially saying that nothing had happened but the new government plan would address the problem. Then, nothing happened.

It begins to get murky at this point. Somewhere along the line Allen Stanford purchased (or agreed to purchase) all the stock in the company that nominally owned Guiana Island, reputed to be around $10 million in some reports and elsewhere for around twice that amount. Since it wasn't a basic fee-simple sale of property, but a stock transfer, it did not appear in Antiguan cadastral records as a real-estate sale, evidently.

Stanford announced yet another elaborate plan to develop the island: He would build 33 sumptuous residences, a golf course, a boat dock and restaurants. The homes would be offered to people of "high net worth," who had, presumably, big boats and played golf. The owners of the houses could berth their yachts at a new marina, to be built on the north of the main island at Barnacle Point, and be delivered by high-speed motor launches to the dock on Guiana Island.

But he needed the acquiescence of the Baldwin Spencer government.

For Spencer and his ministers, it seemed like a workable solution to the mess. The Stanford-acquired company would pay off the government for the original Dato Tan purchase price of just under $6 million, assume the leases on other lands involved in the deal and spend $350 million building the luxury homes, and so on. If you wanted in, you could get a house by joining a sort of homeowners' association at a fee of $35 million and pay $15 million a year for maintenance, etc.

Stanford would toss in the yacht-berthing for free. Environmentalists, in Antigua and from other quarters, went predictably ballistic. But Spencer said Stanford could go for it.

There was another matter no one was speaking about: The property taxes had not been paid on Guiana Island and the mainland acreage since Dato Tan signed the deal years before, and they had compounded themselves with interest and penalties into a hefty sum. The minister of finance, former and apparently then-current attorney for Stanford, Dr. Errol Cort, must have told Stanford, or should have told Stanford, about the tax bill. Some people I talked to in Antigua in 2009 were of the opinion that a secret deal had been made between Stanford and Spencer that the taxes would be forgiven. Indeed, it doesn't make sense to presume otherwise.

At any rate, when the government of Antigua seized Stanford's properties after The Crash, they made no mention of Stanford's having technically purchased Guiana Island. It wasn't until a couple days after the legislature voted to take Stanford's lands that Attorney General Justin Simon, feeling he had a "duty" to disclose the facts, conceded to Stanford's ownership of the island. The problem, apparently, was since it wasn't a recorded deed transfer Antiguan officials failed to seize the island as well. What will happen in this case is up in the air. If the SEC has grabbed all of Stanford's personal assets, then the company that owns Guiana Island is among them and it can be disposed of as the U.S. sees fit. Did Stanford ever pay the taxes? He certainly must have paid what Tan owed on the land, or how could John Fuller's and the Buftons' claims get settled, which they have, according to sources in Antigua? This is yet another legal enigma that should keep lawyers squabbling for years.

After Prime Minister Spencer gave the "green light" to Stanford to proceed with his cockamamie scheme, Stanford for some reason popped up in Spencer's constituency, Gray's Farm, after a woman's house had burned down. Allen spoke publicly of the sad state of the area, its poverty and hopelessness, and pledged to rebuild the woman's house. This was, of course, classic Stanford, the kindly philanthropist. Spencer threw a fit, calling Stanford "arrogant and obnoxious," and changing the green light for the Guiana Island project to bright red. Stanford tried saying he was sorry but got nowhere.

Stanford then embarked on an effort to go around the prime minister, which was a huge mistake on top of his original one. He called it the "I Believe" campaign, showing a 40-minute animated video to anyone who would watch it extolling the infinite benefits to all Antiguans by turning Guiana Island into a rich man's playground. The Antigua public didn't buy it. "Ninety-five percent of the people were totally against the idea," a reporter in Antigua told me. "Stanford blew it big time."

Not a single home was sold to anyone on Guiana Island. Nothing was built, not a piece of sod turned. The marina is dead. Stanford owns an island the U.S. probably can't sell at any reasonable price, since the Spencer administration would be loath to permit the island's development, and in the unlikely contingency that Lester Bird regains power, the Antiguan people and the environmentalists will not stand for his playing ball with anyone over the project. Yet the new taxes will be assessed and will have to be paid, or the Stanford estate will lose every penny ventured in the project. Or, in fact, the investors will lose every penny. Chances are good that is exactly what will happen, given the demise of the Stanford kingdom.

I'll always remember the time Stanford, in one his tirades at a meeting of company heads and lawyers and Stanford executives, sneered, "Bob, you're a great newspaperman, but you don't know a damn thing about business."

Maybe so, but I never would have entertained for a second buying Guiana Island.

8
No way to run an airline

In 1998 Stanford told me he was trying to buy the Caribbean regional airline LIAT, the acronym for Leeward Islands Air Transport [Services]. LIAT was started up in the mid-1950s flying a six-seat Piper Apache twin between Antigua and Montserrat. A few years later, BWIA [British West Indian Airlines], a Trinidad-based, government-owned, much bigger operation, bought up three-quarters of LIAT stock. The new owners added several new planes and expanded its service network. Then in the 1970s the British holiday-charter carrier Court Line acquired the airline, and almost immediately went broke. This was not happy news for the Leeward Islands.

LIAT was then and is now the only carrier with fairly comprehensive coverage of the Antilles. The potential for its collapse rattled the governments of the various island-nations and island-colonies, whose dependence of tourism is vital, as we have seen. Even though tourists never made up the majority of LIAT's passengers, inter-island travel was the carotid artery of the Eastern Caribbean tourism industry. So instead of taking the chance that some entrepreneur, someone who knew how to run an airline, or even another airline company, would pop up to save the day – a phenomenon known as free-market capitalism – eleven Caribbean governments pooled resources to take over the failed company. Many people feared that government management of a traditionally private industry would mean bad service, botched scheduling, mediocre maintenance, union dominance and substantial, perennial losses. This is, of course, exactly what sooner or later would turn out to be the case.

But the management under government control seemed to be doing things right, at least at first. The mismatched mix of equipment was replaced with Twin Otters, rugged short-takeoff-and-landing planes made by de Havilland Aircraft of Canada. By the middle of the 1980s LIAT had expanded its routes to Puerto Rico, the Dominican Republic and other Greater Antilles destinations it had previously ignored. But it still relied on the governments to subsidize its operations, and some politicians were getting flak about throwing money down a hole and wanted out. Facing bankruptcy in 1995, and with only three major government shareholders of any consequence – Antigua, Barbados and St. Vincent – the company sought and got another infusion of capital by selling off about 10 percent of its equity to private interests. It was by then retiring the Twin Otters and outfitting itself with the much larger Bombardier Dash-Eights, with passenger capacities of 35 to 50 seats. But LIAT remained a financial basket case, unable to raise its fares without the permission of the majority shareholders and being squeezed by the unions. The airline struggled along on a shoestring for the next two or three years. But few thought it could ever overcome its funding woes.

The time seemed right for the Stanford Shark Strategy.

The details of what Stanford did next are sketchy, and I report from anecdotes and from reading between the lines of carefully crafted press releases. Stanford is said to have made a magnanimous offer to buy the airline – lock, stock and barrel.

The controlling governments would have none of that, however, which is not surprising to anyone who understands West Indian culture, a tenet of which is to resist selling anything to anybody, especially foreign parvenus with deep pockets. (The Stanford acquisitions in Antigua might appear to put paid to this, but no one ever voted on any of them except Lester Bird and his allies.)

This popular penchant was amply demonstrated when Southern Energy of Georgia made a sweet offer to buy the U.S. Virgin Islands' water and electricity utility WAPA in 1999. The VI Senate shrieked it down, based solely on the fact that "WAPA belongs to the people."

So it does, and the government runs the utility along the same lines as government runs LIAT, egregiously.

So Stanford was getting nowhere.

Rebuffed, Stanford then suggested a big fat loan backed by a major taking, indeed a *de facto* controlling 50-percent chunk, of LIAT stock. Nice try, but forget about it.

That was no way to treat a billionaire, and Stanford rolled his dorsal fin into view. He told us at a later meeting in 1998 that he was going to start up his own airline. At first I thought it was a joke, but Stanford's no comedian. I tentatively raised my hand.

"Uh, say, Allen. You know, the airline business is really tough. I mean LIAT has been in the weeds for decades. BWIA is heading for the shoals. Even United and Continental go bankrupt every couple of weeks, it seems. It doesn't sound like a real good idea."

I got The Look and the open hand slamming down on the table. *Ker-whack.*

"In two years, I'll have put LIAT out of business."

So I reconsidered. It wouldn't have taken much more than a good breeze to blow LIAT over, and if Stanford had concluded that was his objective, it might work. Never mind the staggering amount of capital required to establish a new airline. Stanford obviously had access to that. And since the government of Antigua was in his pocket, even though LIAT was based there, he should be able to wangle the necessary consents on the grounds he would be supplying new jobs and providing better service and all the usual flapdoodle sold to the people to make them happy. Yet, I could not escape the gnawing feeling that Stanford was embarking on the road to a fiscal disaster. But, hell, I don't know a damn thing about business. Just ask Allen.

By the middle of 2000, when I was retiring from the *St. Croix Avis*, Caribbean Star Airline took to the skies. Its fleet consisted of the same Dash-Eight aircraft LIAT was flying; its routes were pretty much the same as LIAT's; its schedule almost exactly matched LIAT's. If LIAT had scheduled a 7:00 a.m. departure from Antigua to Barbados, Caribbean Star left at 7:05. The only notable difference between the two airlines was their fares: Caribbean Star deeply undercut LIAT's.

"He *was* trying to put us out of business," LIAT's then-CEO Mark Darby told me when I talked to him in March of 2009 in his office in Antigua. "The battle was very bloody."

Had Stanford pulled off the shark attack, it still would have come at a cost that might never have been recovered, according to some observers, since the profit margins absent gigantic fare increases could never recoup the money Stanford poured into the maw of such a capital-intensive venture.

"LIAT had suffered many years of problems," Darby said. And, with the advent of Caribbean Star and its predatory designs, both airlines were "losing fortunes."

With LIAT in what Darby called a "death spiral," and Caribbean Star swallowing something like $150,000 every day in losses, the battle wasn't only bloody, it was also mutually destructive, like two boxers close to passing out and still slugging one another in the hope the opponent would fall first. LIAT could stay on its unsteady feet only if the governments that owned it dredged up many more millions of dollars, and they were becoming increasingly reluctant to do so.

By mid-2006, LIAT was still teetering on the ropes, and there was a good chance the governments were going to finally throw in the towel, Darby said. "We wouldn't have gotten any further injections of cash. It was becoming harder and harder to get any more money from them." Earlier that year, LIAT had been able to extract yet another bailout, but it would have in all probability been the last. Referring to Stanford's airline vs. LIAT, "If one of us failed, the other would be saved," Darby said.

For reasons not all that clear to me, but having something to do with air-carrier certification rules about where planes can go, Stanford had started a mirror-image version of Caribbean Star based in San Juan, Puerto Rico, called Caribbean Sun, flying Dash-Eights to places like the Dominican Republic. The certification level that was initially awarded Caribbean Star under Antigua aviation law did not qualify the airline to fly in and out of the United States. That's because the body that sets the civil air regulations in the Caribbean is the Eastern Caribbean Civil Aviation Authority, and the U.S. at the time did not fully recognize its ability to grant airline certifications. So

Stanford cloned the Antigua operation in Puerto Rico, certifying it under U.S. regulations and, by the way, isolating it from the political maneuvering in the islands. Now connections could be made between Caribbean Star and Caribbean Sun to points across the Eastern Caribbean out of the relatively busy hub of San Juan. Seemed like a good idea at the time.

But things went poorly for Caribbean Sun from the day it left the ground in January of 2003 until it perished at age four. There were ample factors that could be adduced in reaching the conclusion that Caribbean Sun was not such a good idea after all. For one, American Airlines, whose system dominates in the Caribbean, has contractual agreements with its American Eagle partner, a huge regional service with a major hub in San Juan flying turboprop ATR twins with a 33-percent higher passenger capacity than the Caribbean Sun Dash-Eights. If you flew American from New York to Antigua, with a connection in San Juan, you would be booked right through to the final destination, and when you came back home, it was American all the way. I don't know if Caribbean Sun had any interline agreements to carry Caribbean-bound passengers from other airlines, but I doubt it.

Another factor is something that had airline executives who noticed it scratching their heads. Stanford planted the corporate headquarters of both airlines in ... Antigua? ... San Juan? ... No, Fort Lauderdale. There were subalterns on site, of course, but the top brass were ensconced in Florida, more than 1,000 miles from the airlines' home bases. Stanford justified this remarkable move by pointing out that the execs had access to Stanford's business jets, which sounded like he had lost touch with reality.

"Frankly, I find it difficult enough managing our business being on-site 24/7," Darby had written on a blog site. "I cannot imagine how he imagined that a complex regional airline could be managed by remote control."

It can't. On January 31, 2007, Caribbean Sun Airlines died in its sleep. The event was memorialized in a press release, which explained,

> Skip Barnette, president and CEO of Caribbean Sun and its sister carrier Caribbean Star, commented on the Caribbean Sun shutdown, saying: "Competition in San Juan has always been very tough, but recent developments have created a no-win situation for us. Major U.S. carriers currently expanding service to the region are increasingly emphasizing nonstop service. The trend toward 'over-flying' San Juan has greatly diminished the strong demand we formerly enjoyed from connecting

passengers. The local market is simply too small to sustain a profitable operation.

Call me bitter and disgruntled, but I don't buy that excuse. What "strong demand" was he referring to? If there was a trend toward "over-flying San Juan," it was certainly not detectable to anyone I knew who did much flying to and from the Eastern Caribbean. Even a few years after the press release blamed "recent developments" instead of R. Allen Stanford for the airline's failure, almost all flights out of, for example, St. Croix to the States stopped in San Juan for a change of planes before going on to the final destinations. I suspect that "recent developments" can be translated as "management blunders," but I could be wrong.

Did I mention that Barnette got his job after Stanford cashiered four of his top airline executives in one day?

Another development, this time real, cited by Barnette was the Federal Aviation Agency's elevation of the Eastern Caribbean Civil Aviation Authority to Category One, authorizing its certification of airlines to a level permitting access to U.S. markets. Caribbean Star was subsequently re-certified, in October of 2006. So the prime reason for Caribbean Sun having been cooked up, in order to get an entrée to stateside destinations, had vanished.

Meanwhile, back in Antigua, during the summer of 2006, with LIAT at death's door and Stanford circling, the two parties started talking about a merger. By the fall of that year, offers and counteroffers were in the air. Stanford was suggesting a "bridge loan" to LIAT of $55 million, for which he would take the 50-percent stake in the new company after the merger. LIAT would be shut down and restarted, perhaps under a new name, maybe Caribbean Star. The LIAT people weren't crazy about that proposal. Stanford said how about 35 percent. Well, that was better, but lending money to a company doesn't usually entail scooping up gobs of its stock. Nonetheless, in a press release dated March 7, 2007, LIAT announced the deal was done:

> The shareholders of LIAT (1974) Ltd. and Caribbean Star Airlines Ltd. announced today that negotiations toward merging both carriers have been finalized. The announcement was made following a meeting held today in Antigua between the Prime Ministers of Antigua & Barbuda, Barbados and St. Vincent & the Grenadines, primary shareholders of LIAT, and Sir Allen Stanford, sole shareholder of Caribbean Star Airlines. Merger negotiations had been ongoing since October 2006.
>
> Under terms of the merger agreement, the Stanford Financial Group will lend the

LIAT shareholder governments a total of US$55 million for the purpose of liquidating LIAT's financial liabilities, as well as to provide working capital. The US$55 million loan will be repaid to the Stanford Financial Group from the proceeds of an Initial Public Offering ....

So the plan was to go public with an IPO? This didn't sound right. Stanford was at all times the sole shareholder of every one of his businesses. "I don't have partners or sell stock," he once told me. "And I never will." Moreover, why would anyone who knew the history of LIAT and Caribbean Star risk a dime buying shares in a new company made up of LIAT and Caribbean Star? I would speculate that Stanford never intended to go public with the new company, but it sounded good to the prime ministers, who were being led down the garden path.

Well, IPO or not, the $55 million loan was to be guaranteed by the governments of Barbados, Antigua and St. Vincent. Some folks wondered why a loan backed by public entities, which made it more or less risk-free, would qualify the lender for more than a third of LIAT's stock. Mark Darby was among the curious.

"I met with Stanford's people on July 7 of 2007 and I asked them why he wanted 35 percent of the stock," Darby said. "What was he really going to get by owning 35 percent? He was not going to have control." It was a good point. And if things had gone Stanford's way, and he bought into the airline through the back door, the rumor mill would have gone into high gear. "Lots of people would have thought there was some sort of inside deal made," Darby said. "And that would have done no one any good."

Stanford and his team apparently agreed. The loan deal was left on the table, but the condition of a stock transfer was quietly dropped. The announcement that a merger had been concluded became null and void. Stanford might have figured he was playing his cards brilliantly, and LIAT, after a few weeks or months, might come begging for forgiveness for Darby's impertinence.

Actually, both sides were bluffing. Both held feeble hands. The hemorrhaging of Stanford's investors' money could not be tolerated any longer. And on the LIAT side, it was pretty clear to Darby and his team that they had seen the last infusion of capital from the governments that owned the company. It seemed certain that if something weren't done quickly, *both* airlines might go under, almost simultaneously. But Darby, as it turned out, knew what he was doing.

Earlier in 2007, Stanford had signed a "commercial alliance" with LIAT, which was a kind of an almost-merger that didn't involve loans or stock transfers. Stanford perhaps saw the deal as the camel's nose under the tent. If so, he had the wrong end of the beast. LIAT took control over Caribbean Star's marketing, sales and reservations. For all intents and purposes, Caribbean Star had become a subsidiary of LIAT. The issuing of the press release announcing the full merger remains a mystery. It never happened.

When Stanford took the stock-for-loan deal off the table, LIAT was laughing up its sleeve. Stanford had been snookered.

"When we took control," Darby said, "it was essentially over."

Stanford's designs, whatever they were, never saw the light of day. LIAT was able to borrow $60 million it by then needed from the Caribbean Development Bank. That money was lent to the governments and given to LIAT. And the bank didn't ask for any stock in return. Stanford was out of the picture.

In November of 2007, Stanford quietly pulled the plug on Caribbean Star Airlines, and that particular high-flying Stanford venture was history.

He sold several Dash-Eight leases to LIAT, thereby avoiding heavy penalties for early termination of the agreements and the associated maintenance contracts, along with some spare Dash-Eight parts, and, more important, Sir Allen saved at least some face. The rest of the planes were sold to the military in the United Arab Emirates, someone told me. It is reliably estimated that

Stanford disposed of around $300 million in his airline fiasco, never to be seen again.

In 2008, Darby said, LIAT was able to turn a modest operating profit. It was perhaps the first time in history that "LIAT" and "profit" appeared in the same sentence.

Darby blogged a cogent observation about Stanford's way of doing business:

> "The 'money-no-object' approach wasn't just restricted to his airlines. All of his businesses were run on a similar basis – perhaps too much 'form' over 'substance'? Certainly anyone who has passed through Antigua can't have failed to be impressed by the manicured 'Stanford-land' enclave (two banks, athletics club, up-scale Pavilion restaurant that it would seem was seldom used by anyone other than Stanford's customers, Sticky Wicket sports bar and private cricket ground) that comprises the approach to the airport terminal. This provided would-be customers of his banks with the impression that here was a solid and credible business."

I couldn't have said it better.

It was not only Stanford's apparent maladroit tactics that got him and his investors sucked into the financial quicksand of an ill-conceived airline gamble, it was also his grievous misapprehensions about West Indian culture. I suppose if you revolve in the heady realms of wealth, zipping around in private jets, dining on *fois gras* (or in Stanford's case, maybe it was upmarket tofu) and caviar, spending hours in board rooms with other rich and powerful men, and if you are accustomed to having sycophants lick your boots, you might not notice how normal people think and act. LIAT survived Stanford's repeated assaults because, among other things, West Indians were emotionally tied to the little airline that their governments, and thus they themselves, owned. They didn't buy the brainless Caribbean Star slogan, "A Whole New Altitude," not because it was a meaningless, lame play on words, which it was, but because LIAT was, in a way, *one of them*. Despite cheaper fares and claims of better service, Caribbean Star was dogged by embarrassingly low passenger load factors while LIAT was at least keeping its head slightly above the surface largely because the average traveler stayed faithful.

Imagine you are a Red Sox fan born and raised in Boston. Will cheaper bleacher seats and a new stadium in the Bronx persuade you to switch your loyalties to the Yankees? No. And that is what Stanford just didn't get.

This business disaster was, unlike a few other dubious Stanford deals that at least had some remote chance of redemption, a dead loss of hundreds of millions of dollars. It can be fairly safely counted as Stanford's costliest mistake. Shortly after Caribbean Star was laid to rest, the wheels of the Stanford juggernaut began to wobble on their axles.

And a little more than a year later, they came off.

9
Stumps, overs and ducks

Cricket is the ancient and hallowed British sport that has been, like the English language, absorbed into the cultural traditions of most of the people formerly or currently under British imperial rule. India, Pakistan, Singapore, Malaysia, Australia, South Africa, New Zealand and the Caribbean are enthralled by the game, just to name a few. Canada is the lone exception, where hockey reigns and baseball is tolerated.

After soccer (football), cricket is the second most-popular sport on earth. Encrusted with recondite rules and curious rituals, cricket is an almost impenetrable mystery to Americans. Lesley, being a Brit growing up in South Africa, knows all about the game and has tried on several occasions to explain it to me. It was like listening to someone attempting to convey the subtleties of Arabic or how String Theory works. What I did learn was that cricket is a sport in which one game, or match, can consume five days with short times out for lunch and afternoon tea. This might be appealing to the English upper classes, which have little else to do with their time, or the unemployed hoi-polloi, but five days seems a bit much for the average sports fan. There is also a truncated version of cricket, known as "one-day internationals" (ODIs) or "limited overs" that can, if necessary, take two days. But I digress.

West Indian cricket is not the stately affair the British are so fond of, with its subdued "Well hit, sir!" and "Good catch!" In the Caribbean, the spectators dance to high-decibel amplified calypso music, scream their approval or disapproval, and have a generally raucous time, aided by beer and rum punch. The English consider all this commotion unseemly, but the passion for the game is as robustly shared.

Eleven players make up a team. There are two batsmen wielding paddle-shaped bats, one at each end of the pitch, the small rectangular center of the playing field where most of the action is. A bowler hurls the ball, made of a cork core wound with string and covered with leather with two raised parallel stitches, to one batter, who stands before three vertical posts (stumps) with two horizontal sticks (bails) resting on top that constitute the wicket. The ball is bounced off the ground a short distance in front of the batsman, who strikes it, if possible, with a sharp uppercut. The bowler is trying to strike any post of the wicket, knocking off one or both of the bails, which puts the batsman out. The batsman is "protecting" the wicket. There are lots of other ways to get out, like allowing the ball to hit your leg (leg-before-wicket, or LBW) or being caught in the outfield or by the wicketkeeper. Once out, another player comes in until the team runs out of batsmen. Since there are two batsmen at all times, the "innings" ends when 10 players are out. In baseball that would be a half-inning. The other team then takes the offense.

After a bowler has tossed six balls, he is replaced by a second bowler. This is known as an "over." In the big international "Test" matches, there might be more than 450 overs, and a single batsman might score a hundred (or more) runs, which is called a "century." The highest Test score ever made by a single batsman was Trinidadian Brian Lara's 400 "not out" in a match against England in 2004.

When a hit is made, meaning the ball isn't caught or scooped up at once, the two batters run in opposite directions to the other end of the pitch, scoring a run from each successful trip where they are able to touch the far batsman's box (the "crease") with their bats before the ball gets there. A ball that reaches the outer perimeter of the field (which is an oval) scores four runs automatically, and a home run (so to speak) is worth six runs, and is called a "six." If a batsman gets put out without scoring a run, it is called a "duck."

The preceding description of the game comprises the bald basics. Any further explanation is beyond my capacities as a cricket analyst. But suffice it to say that the version of the game that Stanford was promoting was a severely condensed one, with a maximum of 20 overs for each team, and thereby called Twenty20 cricket. It was devised in England around 2003 for working stiffs to take in a complete match in the evening after work. Such a match takes only two or three hours. Twenty20, nonetheless, is sniffed at by cricket traditionalists. Its biggest popularity is in India, which has more cricket fans than any other nation.

When Stanford decided to get involved in West Indies cricket, he saw it as yet another way to endear himself to the long-suffering cricket fans of the Caribbean and especially in Antigua. From the mid-1970s to the late-1980s, the West Indian team (familiarly called the "Windies") was arguably the best in the world. The players hailed from 10 countries in the Eastern Caribbean. Most cricketers were black, a source of vaunted pride for West Indian fans, and many were East Indian, from Trinidad and Guyana. The West Indies team to this day holds the record of playing the most consecutive Test matches without a defeat. From 1980 to 1995, the Windies strung together 29 international Test match wins or "draws" in a row. After that era of stunning success, during the late 1990s the Windies fell gradually onto hard times, and by the mid-2000s were essentially cricket patsies. Within this sad state of West Indian cricket Stanford saw opportunity, and he took it.

After he had transformed the Antigua airport with his gorgeous buildings and his vest-pocket Stanford Cricket Ground, finished in 2004, Sir Allen organized a series of cricket tournaments among Eastern Caribbean national teams to be played on his personal pitch. The first event took place in July and August of 2006. Stanford likely didn't know anything more about cricket than the average American, and still doesn't. But that kind of thing never bothered a promoter like Sir Allen. He recognized that the West Indians were to a man deeply depressed about the failed fortunes of the game in the islands. He promised to invest around $100 million over three years, doling out cash to cricket boards, the Twenty20 "board of directors," comprising 13 cricket "legends," to the players and coaches and for prize monies. Stanford claimed his motivation for all this munificence was that athletic excellence should be rewarded. Cricket players don't earn much compared to other professional athletes, and this, Stanford said, was shameful. Even the best English and Australian cricketers get paid a small fraction of what American baseball, football and basketball players rake in. So Stanford, if he was investing and not just spending money, must have envisioned a world in which cricket would draw spectators and TV audiences that would equal or surpass those watching the Dodgers or Knicks or Patriots or Maple Leafs in the United States and Canada. But such a notion would be so far-fetched and laughable that no sentient person would ever come up with it.

Outside of the Caribbean, cricket in the Western Hemisphere is considered an abstruse British eccentricity, regardless of its millions of devotees in the rest of the universe. Even soccer, the most popular game in the world, can't compete with the established North American professional sports. That could be because a typical soccer score is like 1-0 after an hour-and-a-half of fierce running about and kicking and head-butting the ball. As an American pastime, it hasn't a chance. But at least the rules of soccer are pretty straightforward, while cricket is enigmatic at best. A reporter for the *New Yorker* quoted Stanford about his reasons for spending so much money on Twenty20 cricket: "This is the future of the sport. It's only three hours long, it's intense, it will catch the world by storm and off we go to the races."

The Stanford Antigua Twenty20 tournaments were fairly successful, certainly not in revenue, which was not what he was interested in, but in the attention it brought Sir Allen. So he came up with yet another Big Idea: one Twenty20 cricket game with a purse of $20 million.

During the inter-island tournaments, Stanford scouts picked out 17 players who seemed to consistently excel. From those cricketers he gathered together the Stanford Superstars, got Antiguan native son Sir Vivian Richards and some other cricket greats, like Sir Garfield Sobers, then pushing 70, who once was the best all-around cricketer in the world and was knighted by England where he once played (for Nottingham), involved in the $20 million project. Then Stanford started snooping around for a national team to challenge his Superstars. Each winning player would get a million dollars with the rest divvied up among the coaches and trainers. The losers would get nothing.

After being turned down on his bizarre offer by South Africa and some other national clubs, he landed England. He made a deal with the England and Wales Cricket Board for a series of five matches, one each year, beginning in 2008. Despite guffaws from the English press and the indignation of British purists over a Texas cowboy getting his paws into the noble game, the English team came to Antigua with the understandable expectation of routing the Stanford team. With $20 million on the line, broadcast rights were snapped up around the cricket world. The match was played on the evening of November 1, 2008, and the Stanford team gloriously upset the Brits, who batted feebly. Caribbean cricket lovers went wild. The English team lost its stiff upper lip and bawled about the slow pitch, the poor lighting and the fact that the Superstars had had extensive practice on a battleground they had not previously set foot on. They also carped about Stanford's flirting with some English players' wives and girlfriends. Still, the winning players got, after taxes, their gigantic payoffs.

Sir Allen had hit a six. In his mind, reeling from the approbation of the little people, cricket would take the rest of the world "by storm," including America. He even set up some sort of headquarters for Stanford Twenty20 in, of all places, Fort Collins, Colorado. On the Stanford Twenty20 website, visitors were assured that cricket could be easily understood by anyone, and ticked off some of the rules, which gave most readers a headache, or at least someone I know a headache. The idea that Americans and Canadians would embrace the recondite game of cricket was simply preposterous, but then so were most of Stanford's daydreams. But for a brief shining moment, most West Indians believed that Stanford had single-handedly resurrected cricket in the Caribbean. Yet for all the hoopla, Twenty20 is not cricket. And it never will be.

Even so, with the whipped-up jubilation of cricket fans stoked in part by Stanford over the years, the government of the People's Republic of China had handed the Antigua government about $60 million to build the Sir Vivian Richards Cricket Ground in the scrublands of North Sound, a few miles outside St. John's off Factory Road. (As we shall see, Stanford almost certainly had a role in the Chinese granting the money.) The new stadium was erected in time to host the 2007 World Cricket Cup. It also was the venue for two international Test matches, in 2008 (Windies vs. Australia, ending in a draw) and in 2009 (Windies vs. England). But the second of these came seriously a-cropper. The land on which the stadium was set had severe drainage problems, and heavy rains a few days before the February 13 match was to begin flooded the outfield, which groundskeepers tried to repair with an intense application of beach sand. But on the first day of the Test, the players couldn't get any purchase on the soggy ground, and the bowlers had a time of it just running up to the pitch. In a scandalous embarrassment for all concerned, but most particularly the West Indies Cricket Board, the match had to be abandoned and moved to the old, rickety Antigua Recreation Ground, which had been replaced by the new stadium. The match also ended in a draw, another rule of the game that I will not attempt to explain.

Whatever its achievements, Stanford's stab as a cricket impresario was another financial black hole for his wealth-management clients, although the losses were again obscured by the deft use of smoke and mirrors and Stanford's insistent optimism.

It was manifest to anyone paying attention that Sir Allen was doing a great job of disposing of vast sums of money. Where it all was coming from was the conundrum. People who aren't rich naturally assume those who are simply clip bond coupons from time to time or pocket rents from large real-estate holdings or make a killing in the stock market from time to time. And even if Stanford wasn't doing any such things, it would take a long time to go through his reported stash of more than $2 billion. Still, a few doubters predicted that sooner or later something would have to give. They were right.

10
Sir Allen's modi operandi

Sir Allen was interviewed by CNBC's Scott Cohn on the evening of April 20, 2009. It was the first talk with a reporter that Stanford had acceded to since the SEC charges were filed, the other being a confrontational run-in with another TV reporter, who had buttonholed Stanford at a Houston restaurant two weeks before. When the reporter suggested he was running a Ponzi scheme, Sir Allen threatened to punch him "in the mouth." He later apologized for the remark.

In the CNBC interview, Stanford, eyes bloodshot and looking angry and clearly unhappy about having to go on the defense (on the advice of his attorney), responded to Cohn's rather probing questions with evasion and obfuscation, at least in my view. It was redolent of Bill Clinton's denials about Monica Lewinsky, firm and patently misleading, finger wagging. When asked what he had invested his clients' money in and how he could pay returns markedly above those of big banks like Wachovia and Citibank, he said, "You gotta look at our structure. We were in a low-tax jurisdiction. You had one sole shareholder, myself, who was not looking to see benefits for himself ... shareholders were not the primary driving business modi

operandi. It was to get the clients the most money, and that was our modi operandi."

That's where the investments were going? Hello?

"So these weren't fictitious returns, as the SEC claims?"

"Well, there's some things that I found out at a February meeting in Miami that … I've been instructed by my legal counsel not to go into, but, uh, myself as chairman, you asked earlier on what my job was, myself as chairman and shareholder of 42 operating entities around the world employing five thousand people managing billions and billions of dollars, it's impossible for me to macro- much less micro-manage this. I depend on people to do their jobs, which has always been my philosophy as an entrepreneur and the reason I've been successful is to allow people to do their jobs. I stay out of their hair. I set the vision and the goal and certain parameters and let them run their shops."

Well, wouldn't Antigua be somewhere I might want to launder some money? Cohn asked. Didn't he, Stanford, help write the regulations down there?

"Scott, first of all I don't run the bank. I'm the chairman. I have nothing to do with the day-to-day operations. Number two, I did not write the regulations, the banking laws."

Stanford then said that "back in the early 90s" he was asked by the Antigua government, aka Lester Bird, to put together a civilian team of professionals, so "I got [an] ex-FBI, ex-DEA, ex-U.S. attorney ex, uh, uh, person who was head of the commonwealth financing in Puerto Rico, a major accounting firm and others to come up with a strong, if not the strongest, platform for international banking that would meet all the 'know your customer' and other things we were concerned about long before the Patriot Act. And those suggestions were given to the government [of Antigua]. I did not write any legislation. That's another misnomer."

He was asked to update the island's offshore-banking rules and he hired a bunch of retired professionals and lawyers to change the codes and left them to their devices? That was a crock. I was in lots of meetings with these ex-people, and Stanford was the bandleader.

"So you're confident money has never been laundered through your banks," Cohn said.

"You can never say never when you're handling billions of dollars and you're doing this on a routine basis, of course you're going to have something. We had an occasion where you see something happen ...."

Cohn then asked, in view of Stanford's position and his getting to know a lot of people in Latin America, in Africa, and around the world, if he was working with the U.S. government in any capacity.

"It strikes me that someone in your position would be useful to the U.S.," Cohn said, "to try to find out what was going on in places like Venezuela, places like that. Can you tell me about any sort of role that you played in that way?"

"You talking about the CIA?"

"Well, you tell me."

"I'm not going to talk about that."

"Why not?"

"I'm just not going to talk about that."

Stanford said that because of the SEC, he saw his "whole life's work basically vaporize" in front of him. He never said a word about the billions lost by his depositors and investors. His egomania enshrouded him in a cone of silence when it came to the employees who lost their jobs and the retirees who lost their life's savings.

Later, in a tag, Cohn said Stanford told him he made the big returns on smart investing, like real estate and equities. There was some truth in that. Real estate like Guiana Island and Maiden Island in Antigua, mansions in Coral Gables and St. Croix, the airport development that was intended solely, as we shall see, to burnish an image and not for making anyone but Stanford any money, and in retail and office buildings in the Virgin Islands he paid too much for.

The equities he spoke of were private, non-liquid investments, since if he had held big positions in stock-exchange-traded equities he would be losing 40 or 50 percent like everybody else, not providing improbable returns of five or six percent or more.

In the CNBC interview Stanford portrayed himself as a man ruined by the unfounded and vicious attacks of the SEC and the panic that ensued. Stanford was looking for our sympathy, a pitiable victim of the federal government, red in tooth and claw. It was pathetic.

To anyone who ever worked as an executive for Stanford, like me, his CNBC performance was knee-slapping laughable. His assurance that he simply hired the best people he could find and gave them free rein to get the jobs done is pure fiction. He not only macro-managed his companies, he often micro-managed them as well, regardless of his absurd assertions. Implicit in his claims was that his longtime close friend James Davis, the Stanford Financial Group's CFO, was the real miscreant, while Stanford was kept in the dark about Davis's nefarious behavior. So the stage was being set for his defense. It would apparently be a kind of reverse-Nuremberg strategy: Blame the generals, who obviously weren't following his broad orders not to commit any war crimes.

As for the story about writing the Antigua banking regulations, he is accurate in saying "I didn't write" them. No, he dictated them. And it was not in the "early 90s." It was in the late 90s.

The U.S. authorities were putting pressure on Antigua and other offshore sites to tighten up their international-banking regulations if they didn't want to risk losing their ability to work with correspondent banks on

U.S. soil, without which they could not move any money through the global banking systems. (The federal government can withhold, for example, the FDIC deposit-insurance program from any bank it thinks is doing business with shady offshore banks.) Lester Bird and Stanford huddled on the problem, and Bird indeed asked Stanford to put together a team of experts to write new regulations. The team was led by Tom Cash, who (according to my notes) formerly worked for the Drug Enforcement Agency as a special agent specializing in money-laundering and Caribbean offshore banks and at that time worked for Kroll International, a big "risk consulting" and financial-advisory service. The team set up a small office in Nevis Street in lower St. John's.

I was commanded to attend many of the conferences that took place in concocting the new regulations so I could write articles about the developments whenever Stanford thought he needed some good ink.

As I went over my notes recently I was reminded that whatever angles were being discussed, be they couched in obtuse financial jargon or just simple layman's terms, Stanford was directing the rewrite of Antiguan banking laws to make life easier for Stanford.

There were fears that Britain would clamp even further down on the offshore-banking business in the former colonies as it had in extant colonies like the Cayman Islands and the British Virgin Islands and Montserrat. As

Cash pointed out, "If you have to submit to these rules, Stanford International Bank is finished."

There was later a committee of some sort cobbled together to address some of the knottier problems by the Antigua government, and Stanford was one of its members until the U.S. told Lester Bird they didn't think it was a good idea to have a person on the panel who owned the biggest offshore bank in Antigua. Allen graciously dropped out.

There was also a good deal of fretting in these meetings about one Rodney Gallagher, a Briton who had helped reform the offshore laws in the British Virgin Islands and elsewhere in the basin and was probably the most educated man on earth on Caribbean offshore banks. This is the guy Stanford was sure was in the employ of the British spy organization MI6.

"He thinks we're hiding something," Stanford said.

So Allen sent me to Trinidad where a conference was being held by the Caribbean Action Financial Task Force (which, by the way, Gallagher helped create) to see if I could find out what Gallagher was up to. I crashed the private meeting of a hundred or so Caribbean bank-regulation people with a bogus story about losing my credentials in my LIAT baggage, which the guard had no reason to doubt was true. I ran into Gallagher in the lobby, told him I was a reporter for an Antigua newspaper, and asked him some stupid questions. He was affable and even though he could see I didn't know anything about the subject, answered my queries as best he could without laughing in my face. (Gallagher was awarded an OBE in 1998 for his work for Her Majesty's Government in the Caribbean. If he was a spy, he must have been a good one.)

I did learn enough about the subject by attending the seminar that I was able to write a couple of articles on money laundering. In one of them I managed to finger Gallagher as a shadowy character probably working for MI6, as Allen so instructed. For this speculation I received a sternly worded letter of rebuke from the British Embassy in Barbados. (I also found out that Gallagher had been instrumental in booting Stanford out of Montserrat.)

This is how Stanford let his people "run their shops." It was not hard for me to see that I was being used as a cat's paw for Stanford. Despite his protestations of not wanting any editorial control of the newspaper during my interview in Houston, the *Antigua Sun* was Stanford's mouthpiece. The right thing for me to have done was to tell Allen that journalists are not public-relations goons, that I felt morally compromised and was ashamed of myself and wanted to quit. All true, but Lesley and I were ensconced in a foreign country with a leased house, a mortgaged property on which we intended to build a home, a nice salary with good benefits, two cats and no place to go. My ethics got lost, and I did nothing to recover them.

The CNBC interview with Stanford revealed a man standing nearly alone in a world that had turned against him, rightly or wrongly. And even though his characteristic callousness was simmering under the surface, only the most heartless could not feel some compassion for someone who had gone from Master of the Universe to a fretful, defeated financial golden boy whose sorrows were coming, in the words of King Claudius, not as single spies but in battalions. His army of sycophants, his close associates, his allies in the Antigua Labour Party, his former executives, his about-to-be former wife Susan, his cricket "legends" and his worldwide phalanx of money brokers had all abandoned him. When he was rich, he was admired and respected. When he went broke, he was reviled.

But let's go back to that question Cohn posed about the CIA. It took a few seconds, but when Stanford answered, "I don't want to talk about that," I did a double-take. He was, of course, conceding he was indeed involved with the CIA or some other federal entity, and, naturally, he wasn't about to get into details. For conspiracy theorists, this exchange was red meat.

Tyecliffe Castle was a breathtaking 18,000-square-foot Medievalesque manor built by George and Ruth Wackenhut between 1969 and 1974 in Coral Gables, Florida. It was a glorious complex, with turrets and a moat, dozens of nearly priceless stained-glass windows, an Italian garden, a pool made to resemble a forest pond, a clay tennis court and about 100 solid oak doors. The castle comprised 57 rooms and eight baths. It occupied three acres along a

500-foot stretch of a canal in the exclusive part of town called Gables Estates. It looked as if it had been lifted whole from a Bavarian fief in the 1200s and dropped into modern South Florida.

George Wackenhut for decades ran the largest private-security agency in the world. A right-wing ideologue, Wackenhut was a fascinating creature with close ties to extreme anticommunist groups like the John Birch Society. Today, his company, now owned by the Danish firm Group 4 Securicor, which paid $570 million for it in 2002, employs 30,000 or so guards and undercover operatives. It operates in more than 50 countries and collects around $3 billion a year in revenues.

The company's biggest customer is the United States government. Wackenhut security guards work at most of the government's overseas embassies and sensitive critical sites, including the Alaskan oil pipeline, the Hanford nuclear-waste facility, the Savannah River plutonium plant and the Strategic Petroleum Reserve, according to *Spy* magazine. George Wackenhut died on December 31, 2004, at 85, from heart failure.

While never proven nor denied, one of Wackenhut's chief clients was the CIA, according to dozens of articles and books about his exploits.

And a year before his death, Wackenhut's wife Ruth sold Tyecliffe Castle to ... R. Allen Stanford. She was asking $19 million; Stanford paid (just) $10.5 million.

Curious, this. Why would Ruth Wackenhut sell her beloved castle (she orchestrated its construction with European-only craftsmen and artisans bringing most of its materials and decorations from that continent) to Stanford for just over half the price she was asking? Why did Stanford shy at the questions raised by Cohn about his possible ties to the CIA? And why did Stanford, in late 2007 and early 2008, have the gorgeous, unique estate leveled, its interior furnishings, stained-glass windows and the rest, sold off to an architectural-preservation company in West Palm Beach?

Before demolishing the castle, Stanford lived there with his girlfriend Louise Sage Stanford, one of his three "outside wives," with whom he had sired two boys. Although never married, of course, since Stanford was already married to Susan Stanford, Louise Sage adopted his last name and Stanford supported her and the children in lavish style, like European royalty.

Louise and the children left the castle, reportedly, in mid-2004, apparently over some dispute with Stanford. In March of 2008 she sued Sir Allen for child support, who, according papers filed in a Miami court, needed to keep up their "privileged and luxurious lifestyle." Even before the suit was filed, which was settled out of court, Stanford was paying Louise $850,000 annually. Presumably, whatever stipend the settlement called for, it dried up the day Stanford was nailed by the SEC.

Making any connection between Stanford's peculiar answer to Scott Cohn about the CIA and his acquaintance (if he had one) with Ruth Wackenhut is, to be sure, far-fetched yet intriguing. But lots of things about the Stanford saga are far-fetched. Cohn, remember, cited "Venezuela" as one the places Stanford might have knowledge of that the CIA would like to hear about. Did he? Well, one of Stanford's biggest SIB branches was in Caracas. When he was taken down, Hugo Chavez put the bank up for sale.

How about this: Stanford somehow crossed the CIA, and the CIA (it was more likely the DEA) called their colleagues at SEC and asked the latter if they could take him down. Yes, sounds crazy to me too. Alas, we will never know.

11
The Hangar Address

The photos published nationwide in June of 2009 of Sir Allen in an orange prison jumpsuit or in a baggy blue suit, handcuffed and shackled and looking, still, a bit cocksure, were to me as if I had just seen a unicorn or a yeti. They stretched the envelope of belief. The Master of the Universe was in the slammer, sharing quarters with a half-dozen rather more common detainees in a cell stinking of urine and rank body odors.

All Stanford's assets had, of course, been frozen or simply seized in the dozens of jurisdictions they were spread around in. His largely cooked-up fortune of $2.2 billion or whatever was no longer on tap and never would be. To make bail (it was revoked a few days later), Stanford had to call on close friends, family and others. One sound bite had a supporter opining, "I am contributing to his bail bond because I believe Allen Stanford is innocent." Everyone is entitled to his beliefs, but anyone who thinks Sir Allen is "innocent" needs to make an appointment with a psychiatrist.

Regardless of whether the man was convicted in court on any or all the civil and criminal charges brought against him, Stanford's palpable guilt is beyond question.

First, he is a brazen liar. He lied to his wife and his only legitimate daughter about his multiple affairs. He lied to, or caused to be lied to, his tens of thousands of "investors" he bilked unapologetically as he lived a life of extravagance and self-indulgence that would shame the most hedonistic wayward prince or idle heiress. He lied to me, as I have written, including his ridiculous claims made in the letter signed by an underling as my termination notice: a neat dozen demonstrably bogus accusations and ginned-up falsehoods. He lied to the people of Antigua, pretending to be a philanthropist while lending them millions at inflated interest rates, exploiting what was a poor nation to begin with and further impoverished by Stanford's single-handed destruction of its reputation as an offshore haven for foreign money and an Internet-gaming industry presumed by its sucker clients to be carefully regulated and policed. He induced, through various means, officials into compliance with his dubious financial maneuverings.

He is accused of paying bribes to Antiguan and American and other nations' politicians, often disguised as "political contributions." The head of the offshore-banking regulating body in Antigua, Leroy King, was fired and disgraced after it was charged that had taken some $100,000 (see the Appendix) from Stanford in exchange for looking the other way as Sir Allen's bank was pumping in cash from suspect clients, mainly from Central and South America via Florida.

One of the chief sources of cash for Stanford International Bank was his office in a Miami high-rise that employed nearly 50 people. With the aid of a tough and expensive Miami law firm, Greenberg Traurig, Stanford was able to escape the scrutiny of Florida financial overseers by hiding behind a "foreign trust office" veil, with billions of dollars being collected in Miami by Stanford Fiduciary Investor Services and then sent down to Antigua without reporting a dime of it to Florida regulators. This was illegitimate and Stanford knew it. It was not "innocent" by any measure.

Only the most naïve and gullible of those who know him would dispute that he is a rogue and a fraud. We don't need the SEC or the FBI to expose that truth.

There is no need to hypothesize about Stanford's being guilty of a massive con job: He described the scam himself in a telling talk he gave to employees and contractors on June 9, 2005.

Let us set the scene:

In March of the year before, Stanford protégé Lester Bird was turned out of his office as prime minister when his Antigua Labour Party fell to the United Progressive Party of Baldwin Spencer. The UPP had been howling for years about the cozy relationship between Stanford and the ALP. Among many other things, Lester Bird had acquiesced in transferring much of the property surrounding the V.C. Bird International Airport to Stanford during the waning years of the Bird regime. On that property Stanford built his cricket oval, the Sticky Wicket restaurant, Stanford Trust Company (talk about an oxymoron), Sun Printing and Publishing, the tony Pavilion restaurant and the centerpiece, Stanford International Bank.

He had acquired Maiden Island and was trying to acquire Guiana Island. On the former he was going to build a "model mansion" to demonstrate the classy approach to residential architecture to be applied to the Guiana Island development. He had arranged for the government of the People's Republic of China to help finance the construction of a new hospital on St. John's Mount above the town to replace the slummy Holberton Hospital that used to be, and still looked like, a World War II prisoner-of-war camp. He also chipped in about $35 million for the new hospital, tying its repayment to the national Medical Benefits Scheme, which is Antigua's version of socialized medicine. Workers have to contribute 3.5 percent of their pay to the system, which is matched by their employers, guaranteeing the loan would be honored. As it turned out, the construction of the hospital became mired in scandal and consumed something like 10 years to reach completion. The deal with the Chinese was that the PRC would supply 100 or so Chinese workers to build the new hospital at no charge. (At a meeting I attended, when Stanford told Prime

Minister Lester Bird about the plan, Bird said he feared bringing in Chinese workers wouldn't be received well by the voting public, and he was right.)

By June of 2005, Stanford had begun work on a further development at the airport, a complex of hangars for private jets, including his own, and the gentrification of an area on North Sound known as Shell Beach Road and a marina at Barnacle Point not far away. But his relations with Baldwin Spencer's government were testy. The new prime minister was rightfully leery of bedding down with Stanford, as Bird had so conspicuously done, and Spencer had also had contrived a "master plan" for the modernization of the airport, which in some ways clashed with Stanford's ambitions.

One morning in May a letter was delivered to Stanford's offices from the Minister of Civil Aviation ordering Stanford to cease and desist all development at the airport and Barnacle Point "including but not limited to" the hangars and associated projects.

Stanford was livid, but there wasn't much he could do about the *dictat*. He asked for and got a meeting with Spencer, in which he waved money around, his preferred means of persuasion.

This was, apparently, not as effective as he had hoped, so he decided to turn to his 800 or so employees and his non-employee subcontractors in an end run around the government.

He called an "all hands" meeting in the existing hangar, where he had parked two of his private jets and had festooned the walls with artists' renderings of the projects that had been abruptly quashed by Spencer.

About 200 people showed up for the presentation. Stanford, clad in blue jeans and a white polo shirt decorated with his Stanford Eagle pin, spoke to the gathering with a wireless microphone and had the address taped by Antiguan filmmaker Howard Allen, a copy of which I was able to locate. For anyone who has the temerity to charge that Stanford was playing a confidence game, the video is Exhibit A.

After thanking those in the audience for "giving up part of your Saturday," Stanford launched into a rambling speech starting off describing all the wonderful things he had done for Antigua and how he turned the area outside the airport terminal ("which was a cow pasture, a dump really") into what today is what one wag called "StanfordWorld." He went on:

> We have done something over the last 15 years that nobody else in the world has ever done with this airport, to create a unique and wonderful experience. Now, why did I do this? What prompted me to do this? What was the vision, what was the purpose

and why was I willing to spend all the money to do this?

Our core business is financial services. I think all of you know that. Today we have over 5,000 employees in 14 countries. We manage in excess of 25 billion dollars ....

The problem with bringing people in terms of their mind to the Caribbean to do business is the fact that you start out with two strikes against you. People think of the Caribbean as a fun place to go to spend a few weeks, have a couple of drinks every day and watch the sunset go down. But I'm not going to come down there and trust my financial services side of my life to a little island in the Caribbean. Most people say 'no.'

So we have as I like to refer to as two strikes against us whenever we start talking about people doing business with us when we have part of that business domiciled in the Antigua part of the world, in the Caribbean.

So we fly people down here in planes like you see behind you – we have four corporate jets – and we spend our money predominantly in what I call a rifle approach. We go out, target people, work with those people whether they're in our New York office, our Zurich office or the west coast of the states or Mexico or Caracas or wherever it may be, in a way that they feel they are comfortable enough with this organization that we can afford to spend money to fly them to Antigua to see what we're all about.

But when we bring them here we have to give them an experience that is second to none. And when they see things here in Antigua, they can't go back home and say, hey, that was nice beautiful place, the people were friendly and it was a nice visit. No, they have to go back literally blown away. They have to go back literally saying, wow, I saw something there I never expected. I saw people that do things better than they do them in New York or London or Zurich or Mexico or wherever it is we have offices, and I have a confidence and a trust that I will do business in that part of the world.

So, therefore, the Stanford Experience bringing people to Antigua has to be one from the moment they arrive here to the moment they leave here as flawless and perfect and as, uh, impressionable in as many positive ways as we can make it. That is the reason we have an airport development and I was willing to spend millions and millions and millions of dollars on a development that otherwise makes no economic sense. That's the reason you have a Pavilion, that's the reason you have a Sticky Wicket, that's the reason we have the most beautiful grounds around the airport that anybody at any airport has ever seen. That's the reason we're in this hangar right now. That's the reason we want to develop the rest of the property around this old closed-down disused Runway 10 into something that doesn't exist on the planet, so that people of the upper stratosphere of wealth ... the richest people if you want to put it in very layman's terms ... in the world that we bring down here will be impressed and want to do business with us in this country.

I am totally committed to one thing: and that is growing our business in a quality way, which means we are growing our business with what we call high net worth people, and ladies and gentlemen, high net worth people, rich people if you want to call them that, do not get impressed very easily. You have got to do something that is unique in the world, sets you apart in what we call the Stanford Standard of Excellence. That's what all of you are about. Even you sub-trades who don't wear this Eagle Pin are about that. You are about doing something that is better than anybody else is doing this in the world.

Now this leap forward from 15 years ago September to this day, July, what is it, the 9th? 2005, we're sitting in a hangar, two jet airplanes behind you, part of my development in my vision, hopefully our vision collectively, is unfolding, is still beginning to be realized and seen in the flesh so to speak, Barnacle Point over here in the corner, other things at the airport we would like to see happen very quickly, one of them is the Antigua Athletic Club. I'm wearing this shirt today; we want to see that club open in the next six weeks.

Now, when you are moving forward with the program that is 15 years in the making and has involved literally thousands of people and literally several hundred million dollars U.S. of investment on my part, you want to be certain you have a government that is going to be working with you parallel. You're never going to agree with the government on all issues, but it is my belief the government does two things: they make sure that the public safety and conditions thereof are always met by an investor; they make certain that those things that the investors are doing are in an overall master plan the government feels the country should go, and the second thing is the government, in most cases, should get out of the way after they help facilitate the investor to do what he does best, and that is to be a capitalist. That is to invest, that is to employ people, that is to do things that are part of the government's vision and plan. And I thought I had a government's plan that was more or less in synch with what my, hopefully our, plan was.

Now I'm not a difficult person, I don't think, to get along with and I'm certainly not a difficult person in terms of giving things to this country and putting my money where my mouth is and also my heart is. Like me, don't like me, whatever. If I get run over by a bus tomorrow, this hangar we're in, the product that we have produced in the airport, those buildings, and the other tangible things stay in this country. I cannot pick those up and, as one of the ministers of government told me last night, take those things back to Texas. Besides the fact I'm building my home here, umm, for my personal, private primary residence.

I don't intend to pick those things up and take them anywhere; this is a long-term quality investment play in this country. Now if you understand that, if you believe that, and we have a business that is growing by leaps and bounds around the world and I'm putting a large percentage of a portion of that business and the future in this country, then you have a unique opportunity as people that wear this Eagle, people involved with helping us grow that vision among the sub-trades, to be part of something not only unique and special but economically that is one-off in the whole Caribbean and is the biggest thing that has ever happened in this country's history – financially, economically – and will have an impact that truly nobody including myself that has a real understanding of what that positive impact's going to be. If we are left alone to do whatever it is I want to do, within the next 15 months, I will have invested 948 million E.C. dollars [Eastern Caribbean, pegged at 2.7 to one U.S.], of which 450 million dollars of that will stay right here in the pockets of those of you sitting here today, standing here today, and others in the country. That is an economic ripple effect; if you multiply that times three it's about 1.3 billion dollars and that's a conservative ripple effect.

We have – I'm not sure how many – unemployed people in this country, but 3,000 new jobs, 450 million dollars into a sagging, morbid economy is certainly going to do things in this country heretofore never imagined and certainly in the whole Eastern Caribbean; this will be the biggest shot in the economic arm of the country.

That is only one step in much bigger steps if we're allowed to do, again which I'm not going to talk about in detail, the Guiana Island project. All of what we're doing here builds confidence and trust and believability in people we bring here to continue to do business with us and believe in Antigua as a country that we can do things in on a first-world basis. But beyond that I want to bring those people here to spend part of their life. I want to bring some of the wealthiest people in the world to be here a big part of their free time, here in Antigua and a place they will call or hope to call their home. And that's what the Guiana Island development is about. And that's just the first phase of this big vision. That would be a 1.2 billion dollar U.S. continuing investment on top of a 950 million E.C. investment, would continue the employment, would continue to do things that would grow this economy over the next three years in a way that will change all of your lives for the better. All of your lives for the better. It will raise the standard of living in terms of the salaries, it will raise the standard of living in terms of the quality, we will set a standard here hopefully others will want to follow and will bring investors here. In my personal belief it's quality not quantity. We don't want people coming here en masse and don't leave money behind in this economy. We'd rather see a fewer number of people who will spend real money in this economy that affects your lives, your children's lives, our schools, our infrastructure and all of those things that are so critical to a country's growth. We can

make a huge impact, the biggest impact in
this country's future if I have a government
that will work with us.

The translation is easy: The idea is to bring rich people to Antigua in our fancy business jets, squire them around, feed them in five-star style, pour them rare vintage wine and give them a quick tour of our Potemkin Village financial-management offices, and all that's needed thereafter is to reel them in. They will think we are hugely successful and eagerly hand us their money to get outlandish returns. To plenty of fish, this was a transparent and audacious con job, and they weren't sucked in. But to many others, it worked like an Irish charm. And it explained, that is to say Stanford explained, the reason for all the lavishness and overwhelming extravagance of everything he built and said and how he decorated his offices and how he bought (and leveled) multi-million-dollar estates to remake in his "vision." It was all an elaborate and wildly improbable diversion. It was, regardless of what Stanford believed or pretended to believe, a confidence job on steroids.

Thus his speech that day was intended to mobilize his workers and his contractors to somehow bring political pressure to bear on the island's government so they could have their lives improved through Stanford's translucent manipulations and pretenses.

Incredibly, a Texas bumpkin with a bachelor's degree had so far succeeded in a vast and inspired charade. He knew, to his everlasting credit, that rich folks were among the easiest to lure into the net by playing on their intrinsic greed. See, he said, I'm one of you. I've got all the material things that wealth brings. My name is Gatsby. Put it there, pal. Next?

One of the victims of the Stanford Experience was a woman, Rosa Mejia, whose elderly father handed $400,000 to a Stanford broker in the company's plush Miami offices for a certificate of deposit worth nothing. When she discovered every penny was lost, she was shocked.

"Everything was first class," she said. "We thought our money was safe."

12
Where da money gone?

From the Houston *Chronicle*, July 9, 2009:

The lead British receiver fighting for control of assets related to the offshore bank at the center of the alleged $7 billion Stanford Financial fraud said Tuesday he expects whatever bounty is found won't reach $1 billion.

"The bank has no cash whatsoever," Nigel Hamilton-Smith said in an interview. "The bank took in money and invested it. And the assets at the bank, in my view, are going to realize less than $1 billion — and potentially significantly less."

He said the value of certain assets is "wholly, wholly uncertain." Those include undeveloped islands the bank bought last year for $63.5 million, then transferred to other Stanford entities that sold them back to the bank for more than $3 billion.

Pretty neat trick. Buy lots of real estate with investors' funds. Transfer the properties to "other Stanford entities," and inflate their value from $63.5 million to more than $3 billion and sell them back to Stanford International Bank. Now SIB has on its books real estate with a concocted value of $3 billion. This is a violation of generally accepted accounting practices, and was one of the ploys used by Kenneth Lay's Enron, called "mark-to-model." Stanford based the pumped-up value of the land and islands on what he *planned* to develop, not on what they were in fact worth, which happened to be even less than the $63.5 million he (or rather his bank) reportedly paid for the properties in the first place.

Who owned the Stanford International Bank in toto? Sir Allen Stanford. So he, in effect, increased his "net worth" by nearly $3 billion. Indeed, one of Stanford's "modi operandi" was to own everything, every branch of every business. They were all "wholly owned proprietorships," in the words of one of Stanford's lawyers during my tenure in Antigua. He had no partners, no one to answer to, no actual board of directors, no stockholders. Despite his protestations to the contrary in the Scott Cohn interview, Stanford not only managed every aspect of his suspect operations, he also was the only one who knew exactly what was going on.

When he "bought" Guiana Island, he actually acquired the company that owned the island, Dato Tan Kay Hock's Asian Village Antigua Ltd. "Apparently," according to the *Stabroek News*, "Asian Village was found to be incorporated in Tortola, the shares of which were held by another company registered in the Isle of Man, held by yet another company in the Isle of Man, whose shares are owned by Allen Stanford."

Stanford's one-man-band ownership of all these various entities says much about his business strategies, but it says even more about the man himself and his ultra-narcissist psychological problems.

A blogger who calls himself the "New York Crank" writes:

> As some of my more faithful readers know, I'm an ad guy. Around 2005 I was doing work for a small Manhattan ad agency ...They were pitching a new client. For a rather small agency, he was big business. I mean BIG.
>
> "He's gonna spend at least five million bucks with us the first year," gushed an account management guy, who turned out to be painfully wrong.
>
> "He," was R. Allen Stanford, a Texas (of course) investment banker who now turns out to be a second-string Bernie Madoff.
>
> Stanford told some agency people he was closely related to the founder of Stanford University. He evidently has told other

people, too. (Not true, the University insists, turning around and launching a law suit against good ole boy R. Allen for trademark infringement.)

When R. Allen showed up at the agency, he ordered the entire staff lined up for him to meet. No, not a hand-shaking kind of thing. More of an inquisition.

"What do you do here?" he asked, glaring at a terrified looking woman. "And you, what do you do?" he demanded of another victim.

He didn't ask everybody. He didn't seem much interested in the answers, either. Instead, he seemed hellbent on impressing on everybody that he wanted respect, damnit. Groveling, bootlicking, kiss-his-butt respect.

Stanford told us that he puts on a conference every year in New York, using space at a particular Manhattan hotel. "I spend $300,000 a year there, so I think I'm entitled to have everybody who works there know my name," he said. He seemed to me to be impressed with himself. And proud.

Evidently, the entire hotel staff was briefed by their panicked management. Hundreds of people, including frequent repeat customers, come and go. But that guy with the goofy mustache, whenever you see him, it had better be "Good morning, Mr. Stanford." Or "Good evening, Mr. Stanford." Or else.

So one day good ole R. Allen walked into the news shop in the hotel lobby. The clerk there didn't say, "Good morning, Mr. Stanford, Sir." She just hands him the newspaper he asked for.

"Do you know who I am?" he asked her.

"Nope," she said with a shrug.

Explosion! R. Allen Stanford, nearly in meltdown state, went to the management of the hotel and demanded to know why the clerk in the news shop didn't know his name.

"The shop isn't part of the hotel," the manager explained. "They just rent the space from us."

That was no excuse for R. Allen Stanford, who wanted things changed fast or there was going to be a $300,000 annual loss of business to pay.

Mind you, R. Allen Stanford told this story on himself, to a roomful of strangers.

In one incident, Stanford seemed reminiscent, at least to the *Antigua Sun* staff, of the neurotic Captain Queeg in "The Caine Mutiny," who makes a huge fuss over the disappearance of a quart of frozen strawberries. We had sent a Nikon camera to New York City for repairs, carried north by a woman we knew who lived in the city and who had dropped the camera off at a shop there. Stanford demanded to know who had the missing camera, and if it had been embezzled or otherwise illegally diverted. The Nikon was worth no more than a couple hundred dollars, but memoranda flew, angry phone calls were exchanged and Stanford was making a complete fool of himself. We finally had a receipt from the repair shop faxed to Stanford's office, and the matter was dropped. But it had everyone shaking his head in disbelief.

And speaking of micromanagement, one day Stanford stopped by the newsroom and noticed that my desk was not covered with glass. He demanded to know who was responsible for this intolerable oversight, could not identify a miscreant, and barked out an order to have the desk covered immediately. To be consumed by such trivia seemed to us an indication that R. Allen Stanford was a few cards shy of a full deck.

In study after study of successful men and women, the virtues of hard work, self-effacement, traditional morality and a well-grounded responsibility to investors – whether stockholders or lenders – are paramount. Stanford failed chiefly because he adhered to none of these virtues. Instead of making sure his employees, be they ditch-diggers or top executives, were doing their jobs, by his own contention he didn't "get into their hair." He said he believed that by engaging "the best of the best" he could rely on others to supply the talents he himself lacked. Trouble was that he *did* get into their hair, but mostly in matters that were trivial or personal, not strictly business-related. He once admonished one of his most capable executives, who had the audacity to light up a cigarette at a company Christmas party, saying, "We'll cure you of that." As we have seen, it was more important to Stanford that all employees displayed the Stanford Eagle pin than whether the person was doing a good job and helping to make good returns on investors' money. The executives were, for all intents and purposes, place-holders, while behind the scenes everything was being manipulated by Allen Stanford.

His flamboyance and desperate need to appear rich and powerful, a need that permeated nearly everything he did, was the antithesis of self-effacement, and his shameless womanizing ran hard against his Baptist upbringing and revealed the hypocrisy of his claims to morality and compassion. His fleecing of investors and the sea of lies required to keep the boat afloat amplified his utter disregard of those who were unlucky enough to trust their money to his care and of the employees who worked so long and hard for him.

The only thing that ever mattered to R. Allen Stanford was R. Allen Stanford. He even turned viciously on his longtime friend and Stanford Financial Group chief financial officer Jim Davis, a man not entirely free of personal peccadilloes but at bottom a good-hearted gentleman who feared God even more than he feared his boss. When Stanford was finally cornered by the feds, he was quick to blame any irregularities on Davis, whom, he said, he trusted and who failed him. It was not surprising that Davis chose to cooperate with the investigators to save whatever skin he could.

Stanford's vaunted notions about himself so obscured his grasp of the truth that anything that went wrong was always, *always,* someone else's fault. It was the *Antigua Sun* staff that was culpable for the newspaper's lack of profits. It was a broker in Houston that got the bank involved with shady Mexican money-launderers. It was his team of airline-business executives that ran Caribbean Star into the ground. It was the vindictive government of Antigua that sunk his ambitions to continue development of the airport. It was the SEC that destroyed his empire and his life.

His habit of cashiering anyone who displeased him in the slightest without regard for the consequences of that person's sudden banishment never seemed to give him pause. As the then-captain of Stanford's 120-foot Sea Ray motor yacht said to me a few days after I went to work in Antigua, "I have seen Allen fire people at the drop of a hat. And believe me, it ain't pretty."

Nearly two years later, I was to find out just how accurate that statement was.

128

13
The curtain falls

In the late summer of 1998, Stanford summoned me to the house he leased in Antigua and introduced me to a new employee, a woman named Linda Wingfield. He announced that Ms. Wingfield would now be his "eyes and ears" on the island and I was to be stripped of my functions as the *Antigua Sun's* general manager and would now serve only as editor-in-chief. That I was essentially being fired was obvious, but since no one was around to take my place, the dismissal would be transparently postponed.

Wingfield, who can be described charitably as someone whose caloric intake had clearly outstripped her metabolic rate for many years, had been brought aboard by Stanford after what he said was a rather brief interview in the cabin of one of his business jets parked in Houston a couple of days before. She knew nothing about the newspaper business, nothing about Antigua or the Caribbean in general and little or nothing about Stanford. But, as I suspected, she knew plenty about hatchet work.

Wingfield began visiting the *Sun's* offices nearly every workday as the weeks went on. She interviewed all the employees in closed sessions. She pored over the books. She grilled me time and again on topics she had little grasp of, asking mostly absurd questions and getting equally absurd answers. At one point she breathlessly swept into my office waving some documents.

"You claimed this project made a profit," she growled, "and it really lost thousands."

It turned out she was talking about a hurricane-preparedness booklet we had produced some months before at the start of the hurricane season (which runs from the first day of June until the last day of November). This kind of publication is staple stuff – or was at least before the immense popularity of the Internet – for the various Eastern Caribbean newspapers, either as a supplement or a separate publication.

Along with a tracking map, readers get lots of details about how hurricanes begin, what to do when a storm is heading one's way, what to stock up on and what to do as the tempest passes. Typically, these publications are fairly rich in advertising and are usually distributed free of charge.

As I recalled, we had made a modest profit on the project. I therefore had no idea how Wingfield could have concluded we lost money.

"Look," she said. "With the production, printing, commissions and shipping, you spent [something like] $50,000. But the total ad revenue was only $45,000. That's a dead loss of $5,000. Mr. Stanford is not going to be happy about this."

Forget that $5,000 would be to Stanford little more than chicken feed. The problem was, as far as I could gather, that I had misled my superiors. Had I miscalculated the results? Had someone made an error in simple arithmetic? What the hell was going on?

Wingfield tossed the documents onto my desk. "What do you have to say?"

I looked over the report, scratching my head. I soon realized what had happened: Wingfield had mixed up U.S. dollars with Eastern Caribbean dollars. She had reckoned both the income and the expenses in U.S. currency, but in fact the expense figures had been expressed in E.C. currency while the revenue (since most of the ads came from Trinidad-based agencies) was paid in U.S. dollars. Thus the advertising amounted to U.S. $45,000 and the outlay, in U.S. dollars, was only about $18,500.

I couldn't be sure whether she realized how her ignorance and unfamiliarity with Eastern Caribbean dollars made her look like an ass, but I hoped so. I gently explained the error.

"Well," she said. "You had better make sure this is made totally clear in the future," or something lame like that. And she left.

In retrospect, this incident might have so embarrassed Wingfield that she silently vowed to work even more tirelessly toward the goal of delivering my head to Stanford on a platter.

Whatever the reasons, that's pretty much what she ultimately did.

Since I had some vacation time in the bank, I thought it would a good idea to take it. The day before I was to leave, Wingfield scheduled an "interview" with me in my office. She peppered me with questions that left little doubt she was preparing a bill of particulars against both Lesley and me. As a precaution, I had my assistant Jane George-John attend the interview and take notes. It was Jane, ever with her ear to the ground, who had warned me several days earlier to "watch your back."

I went down to Trinidad where I thought I might combine some idle time with visits to a few ad agencies. I was there two days when I came down with a wretched case of food poisoning, the symptoms of which I shall decline to detail. I spent the next three days in the hotel room consuming chicken soup and orange juice courtesy of room service.

After a couple days on my back, Linda Wingfield phoned alerting me that "Mr. Stanford" wanted to know when I would be returning to Antigua. She either did not sympathize with my affliction or, more likely, thought I was faking it. She insisted I come back as soon as possible. Things began to get curious, and then bizarre.

I flew back to Antigua on a Sunday evening and soldiered my way back to the office Monday morning. When I arrived, a uniformed guard roughly the size of a

Honda Civic blocked the entrance to the office suite and demanded I say my name.

"My name is Hoffman. I'm the editor."

"You're not on da liss," he said.

"What list?"

He waved a piece of paper. Then he extracted a photocopy of the paper's masthead on which my name and Lesley's had been highlighted.

"I hab bin tole not to permit you to entah," he said.

Had the man been, say, 200 pounds lighter and stood ten inches shorter I might have pushed him aside. But under the circumstances that did not seem a prudent strategy.

So I retreated and walked a half-mile to the Human Resources office in a little professional center just east of Woods Centre. There I confronted Mona Quintyne, the head of that division, who had no idea what I was talking about.

She made some quick phone calls.

"Uh, apparently Mr. Stanford wants you and also Lesley to take another week of vacation. You have not been fired."

"Well," I said, "barring me from going into my office seems a remarkable way to convey that."

Mona shrugged.

Since my bout with bacteria had ruined my first week in Trinidad, Lesley and I decided to go back down, where she had longtime family friends and I could try to dredge up a few ads for the *Sun*. So off we went on what was essentially a suspension with pay.

When we returned to Antigua a week later, I found under the door to my house an envelope bearing the Stanford Financial Group return address. In it was my termination notice, backed up with twelve grounds for my dismissal, every last one of which was patently false.

I have never been able to fathom quite why Stanford turned on me and Lesley (who lasted maybe two weeks longer in her managing-editor job) with such venom. If he wanted to replace us, all he had to do was call us in, offer us a reasonable settlement – since our employment contracts were for five years, and we had been with the *Sun* just short of two – and we would have gone on our way. But, just as the yacht captain had warned me, when Stanford goes after you, "It ain't pretty."

H.G. Helps, one of our best reporters at the *Sun* whom I had hired as a sub-editor in 1998, wrote a piece in the Jamaica *Observer* (where he now works) a few days after Stanford's collapse. He described how he and Louis Daniel met their ends at the paper shortly after Lesley and I were canned. One evening he came into the newsroom, where then-acting editor Daniel was on the phone with Stanford. Daniel switched on the speaker phone:

"I have been receiving complaints
from the Government members that the Sun

has not been co-operative and kind in highlighting the work of the Government and we need to do something about that," [Stanford] said before ending the conversation abruptly.

That was the start of a dramatic turn of events that would follow.

As the general election campaign got into full force, the words flew left, right and centre. The Opposition always expected a bashing from the paper, based upon its owner's connection with the Government. It did not happen often and the paper's credibility grew slowly.

But the Government was growing uneasy that for once in the short life of the Antigua Sun, the playfield had leveled off and the paper was by no means a State mouthpiece.

But for how long would that last?

Following a short vacation to Jamaica around Christmas time, my trip back to Antigua in January was eventful.

The election campaign had gathered heat, the Government was giving away land to citizens at peppercorn rates, offering every adult the opportunity to import a vehicle duty free and promising just about everything that it could, in a bid to excite voters. For its part, the Opposition bashed the latest attempts at winning over the uncommitted.

Stanford seemed to be perspiring profusely every time he viewed the situation, which showed the Opposition gaining ground. Something had to be done to keep voters focused on the ALP.

Presto! Stanford had a bright idea. He [had] promptly fired the Hoffmans and made Daniel the interim editor. Daniel would last a short time, as Stanford had specially imported a retired Trinidadian newsman called Vernon Khelawan who was expected to lead the charge in 'transforming' the Sun to reflect a more sympathetic attitude toward the ruling party.

More and more stories, most written by Khelawan, made their way into the paper. If there was a story that would make the Opposition look good, it was either not carried right away, or at all. Anything that would show up the UPP would make the front page or get other prominent places in the paper.

One Saturday afternoon I was asked by Daniel, who had been relegated to news editor, to cover an Opposition rally near the Antigua Recreation Ground. Former journalist and [UPP] deputy party leader Tim Hector had made one of the most brilliant speeches that I had heard from any Caribbean politician in recent times.

As there was no publication on Sunday, I wrote the story the day after. Daniel was at the office and we decided that the story would lead the paper for its Monday edition.

We left the paper's offices around 8 o'clock that night and close to 11 o'clock I got a call from Daniel that Khelawan and a Guyanese/Antiguan diplomat, who was working with the Bird Government at the time, had gone to the office when most people had left and not only changed our front page but other sections of the paper.

The story, which had been critical of proven Government corruption, including a U.S. $11-million airport development project for which money was paid out in full to a Government member and only two truck loads of sand delivered, was removed from

Page One, dumped and replaced by a story highlighting the achievements of the Government. Other stories that had no political connection were also yanked from the paper and replaced with Government handouts.

At dawn, when most of the staff had reported to work, an emergency workers' meeting was called and a decision made to proceed on a sickout, until the company's management stated the reason for the changes. The sickout lasted two days, and when the workers turned up on the Wednesday, so did Stanford. He hastily called a staff meeting at which he huffed and puffed and almost blew the house down. He singled out Daniel and myself for leading a rebellion against what he called the protection of his interests.

Stanford lambasted Daniel in his usual style. When it came to me, he looked me up and down for what appeared to be hours, then in a terse manner said, "I want you to take some time off from work. But I will pay you, I will pay you," he emphasized. "I think you should take the time to examine your hearts and minds and then decide whether or not you want to continue working for this company."

So we received our marching orders and by later that day the news that Stanford had suspended us had attracted the attention of the major media organizations, including the BBC Caribbean Radio, television stations, newspapers, the Caribbean Association of Media Workers led by Rickey Singh, the Press Association of Jamaica headed by Desmond Allen, the Media Association of Jamaica led by Chris Roberts and diplomatic missions on the island.

That infuriated Stanford even more. How dare two poor boys take him on and attract this kind of attention. His next move was inevitable. Stanford gave the orders to dismiss us and in less than three days that took effect.

Thus two of the finest journalists in the Caribbean were shown the gate for being journalists.

My termination notice was signed by Mona, a competent, gentle and generous woman who ultimately also got sacked by Stanford. She had been ordered (we later learned) to issue the notice over her signature, but it had been wholly concocted by Wingfield and Stanford. It was obvious Wingfield relished her role as the executioner, but otherwise nothing made sense to me (until I heard about the sacking of Helps and Daniel).

Mona, understandably, declined to discuss the matter with me under pain of punishment for violating company policy.

A few days after my departure, I got a phone call at home from Allen.

"Bob," he said, "I don't understand how you could screw up the best thing that ever happened to you. You know, I sent someone down to check on your doings in Trinidad. Why were you were working against me?"

Talk about paranoid.

Anyway, as I responded to that audacious and preposterous remark about the "best thing that ever happened to me," I told Stanford that I of course knew he had sent a spy to Trinidad. I did, after all, have quite a few friends on that island.

"Yeah, he's a lawyer," I said, "and he stayed at the Holiday Inn in Port-of-Spain for three days making phone calls. And he found nothing untoward about me or anyone connected with me, and you are, or should be, well aware of that. Whoever is giving you information is dead wrong."

"Have a good life," he said. And hung up.

At that point, Lesley had not been fired, mainly because Wingfield and Stanford had yet to come with a plausible excuse to justify it. Then someone had a truly dumb idea: Make Lesley the "Barbuda editor."

Barbuda is the sister island that lies about 25 miles due north of Antigua. Nearly all of its 1,500 inhabitants live in the town of Codrington. The flat terrain consists of coral limestone mostly covered with low bush. Its highest point is just over 100 feet, and its mangrove swamps are home to more than 2,000 frigate birds. A few feral goats, horses and donkeys wander around undisturbed by tourists, of which there are few. Barbuda has just two smallish hotels, both of which are expensive and exclusive retreats for the rich and famous. If anything of consequence has ever happened on Barbuda, I can find no record of it. Thus assigning Lesley as the "Barbuda editor" was intended to be some sort of humiliating demotion that Wingfield and Stanford assumed would persuade Lesley to quit. If so, they were wrong again.

Lesley enthusiastically accepted the new arrangement, which was to require her to spend at least two days a week on Barbuda, gathering breaking news and reporting on significant developments. She asked for a camera, playing the inane game with tongue in cheek. Perplexed that the transparent ploy was turning into an embarrassment, Stanford came up with a better strategy. He fired her.

Stanford refused to pay either Lesley or me for unused vacation time, severance pay, expenses due to be reimbursed and even straight salaries he owed us. We sued him under Antigua law, won both cases and, after he appealed every decision and lost, we eventually collected enough to make us feel the effort was worth it, despite most of the money having gone to our lawyer and spent on travelling to and from Antigua for several court appearances. Helps and Daniel also sued and also won.

No matter that many people – Stanford's father James, CFO Jim Davis, Antigua government officials, editors of a couple of other Eastern Caribbean newspapers and various local readers – went out of their way to compliment me and Lesley and our great staff for the quality of the *Antigua Sun*, Stanford shot us all like rats in a dump. Everyone, well, almost everyone, was baffled.

Wingfield had confirmed widespread suspicions among Stanford workers that she was a hired gun. The morale at the newspaper and other Stanford holdings went south as Wingfield scouted around for her next targets. Some of the *Sun* reporters and sub-editors quickly began looking for more secure places to work, and within a few weeks she had taken care of Helps and Daniel as well.

By extraordinary good fortune and maybe even through the kindly hand of Providence I was able to land a job as Eastern Caribbean correspondent for the Associated Press in, ironically, Trinidad, to which we soon repaired.

A year later, I became editor of the *St. Croix Avis,* preferring to return to United States soil after three years in foreign countries where you never know if and when the authorities might conclude your privilege of residence should be withdrawn.

Our affection for Antigua nonetheless endures, despite the tribulations and disappointments. In March of 2009, I spent a week in that little country, meeting old friends and former coworkers and remembering the good times we had there. When I popped in unannounced at the offices of the *Sun*, Adelpher Browne, the receptionist I had hired 11 years before, leapt to her feet. "Bob! How are you, my dear?" It was touching and a bit sad. At that moment, Sir Allen had been charged by the SEC and was about to be indicted for fraud. Without Stanford's cash faucet, the paper seemed headed for extinction and all the good people who were left would be, like hundreds of other Stanford workers, on the street.

"What's going to happen?" I asked Adelpher.

"Oh," she said. "We're just going day to day. With Mr. Stanford, you never know."

No, you don't. More than 800 Antiguans and expats on the islands were left with nothing after years of loyal service to the man, who could not bring himself to utter a word of apology.

Antigua's reputation as an offshore banking venue was in the pits, and a lawyer representing thousands of Stanford investors in July of 2009 had filed a lawsuit against the Antigua government that sought damages in the billions of dollars. For all that Stanford claimed to have done for that country, he had inflicted enormous injury on it, all without remorse or regret.

In a just world, it is the people of Antigua who should be seeking redress – from the U.S. federal government and from the states of Florida, Texas and others that allowed Stanford to recklessly plunder people's fortunes and for misleading nearly everyone into buying his deceptions and for stoking the corruption that so often infests the weak and naïve nations of the Caribbean.

But, at bottom, Antigua and other islands have had an old lesson reinforced: Beware of slick outsiders bearing gifts. They often turn out to be false prophets with little other motive than to exploit their gullible hosts.

Not all the people who see opportunities for investment in the Caribbean are swindlers. But those who are poison the water and tar the innocent with presumed dishonest intent.

The governments, of Antigua and other Eastern Caribbean islands, are not free from culpability. In many of these jurisdictions, the soil is fertile for corruption, tax evasion and other wrongdoing.

When things go badly, they cannot put the blame on the perpetrators alone.

Antigua has a lot of work to do in repairing its reputation, which wasn't all that good even before Stanford arrived on the island. And Sir Allen could have never pulled off what he did without the almost total compliance of the authorities.

The current rulers in Antigua have been quick to attempt to take political advantage of the disaster by pointing to the misdeeds of the Antigua Labour Party and the Bird family in causing the Stanford Experience to occur. This, of course, has some grounds in reality, but the United Progressive Party and its allies were not all at sea during the Stanford years. They were the main opposition, and they failed to ring the tocsin loudly enough before it was too late. Antigua needs a thorough political house-cleaning, and that is now job number one for a new generation of Antiguans.

The political class in Antigua is chiefly a collection of recycled old men, connected cronies and relatives. Attempts at reform are traditionally doomed at birth as the two main parties simply trade places from time to time as the corruption, patronage, nepotism and politics-as-usual endure, stoked by a bloated public sector that represents a reliable voting bloc. It will not be easy to dislodge the entrenched interests, perhaps impossible. But if the Antiguan people can dredge up the courage that it will take, a new dawn might someday break.

Stanford and his money tree are gone. The legend of Papa Bird is fading from memory. Has the time now come for Antiguans to once again declare their freedom? I devoutly hope so.

14
Houston, we have a problem

On February 2, 2009, just two weeks before Sir Allen Stanford was shot down by the SEC, a U.S.-based financial analyst named Alex Dalmady published an article in a Venezuelan newsletter, *VenEconomy Monthly.* VenEconomy is, according to the Latin American *Herald Tribune*, "Venezuela's leading consultant and publisher on financial, political, and economic issues." In his amusing but devastating report, Dalmady concluded that Stanford International Bank of Antigua was perpetrating a fraud. In fact, he wrote, it looked a lot like a Ponzi scheme. Applying the ancient saw that if it waddles, quacks, has a flat beak and feathers, it just might be a duck,

According to SIB's financial statements, as of the end of 2007, 42 percent of its portfolio was invested in stocks, 20 percent in fixed income (bonds), 25 percent in hedge funds and 13 percent in precious metals.

Dalmady explains:

> That is a relatively typical allocation
> for this bank and over the last few years it
> has gone from a low of 27% in stocks (2004)
> to a high of 60% in 2006. Nothing to see here,
> right?

How about this? The return on the portfolio over the last years: 2003: 14.4%, 2004: 11.5%, 2005: 10.3%, 2006: 11.0%, 2007: 11.4%. Can you see a pattern emerging? One of consistency. Considering only the stock portfolio, the returns were: 2004: 8.2%, 2005: 8.8%, 2006: 11.7%, 2007: 8.2%. Nothing out of the ordinary, right?

Consider the returns on the S&P 500 the same years: 2004: 9%, 2005: 3%, 2006: 12.8%, 2007: 3.8% (we'll talk about 2008 later). The bank did quite a bit better than average. As for other categories, they report a 22% average annual profit on their hedge funds and 12% on precious metals. Not bad at all.

[SIB] takes its name from owner Sir Allen Stanford, a Texan billionaire and cricket aficionado ... He was recently named *World's Finance* [a U.K.-based magazine] "Man of the Year" for 2008.

For those who may not know, 2008 was an awful year for investing. The S&P had its worst performance since the Great Depression, falling 38%.

Few investment categories weathered the storm. For stocks, corporate bonds, commodities, currencies and/or hedge funds, it was all pretty bad.

In a Nov. 28 note to its depositors, the Stanford International Bank acknowledged that it had performed poorly. But just "a little" poorly. They acknowledge a $110 million loss up until that date (a quarter of the equity). Doing a little math, that doesn't mean that the bank's investment portfolio lost money (like almost everyone). It means that they didn't profit enough to get back to break even. Since the bank invests the money of its depositors and has to pay them interest plus the commissions to its affiliated advisors, it must earn at least 8-9% on its investments in order to compensate these costs. The bank is recognizing that in 2008, the year of the great crash in the markets, it "only" made a 5-6% return on its portfolio. Quite an act of contrition.

Dalmady's article was by no means the first time questions had been raised about Stanford's banking empire. During the first few years of the decade, former employees and erstwhile broker/agents affiliated with SIB and Stanford Financial Group had blown whistles to the SEC, following which the SEC, as bureaucrats are wont to

148

do, did nothing. But the noise was getting more constant and louder, so the SEC did a little snooping around and concluded that even if the Antiguan branch of the Stanford Experience might be up to something, it was not within its jurisdiction. Besides, the Antigua officials were quick to assure the SEC that everything about Stanford and his bank was legitimate.

However, the Dalmady attack seems to have been the last straw. In the wake of the financial carnage authored by Bernie Madoff, the U.S. authorities were not going to get burned yet again, and they lowered the boom. In defense of the SEC, it appears that the Department of Justice had asked the former to hold off on any investigation of Stanford since the FBI was conducting a criminal probe and didn't want its case compromised by a big civil suit. Had it not been for Madoff, Stanford might have lasted at least a little longer.

Another serious complication for the Stanford juggernaut was the loss of the Antigua Labour Party to the United Progressive Party in the March 2004 general election. Without the generous compliance of Lester Bird as prime minister, Sir Allen and his Antigua interests were severely squeezed. The new administration of Baldwin Spencer could not simply hand Stanford his walking papers, since there were hundreds of jobs at stake and no politician could survive putting that many people out of work in order to exact revenge for Stanford's financial support of the ALP and the Bird regime. Still, Spencer was not going to fall into lockstep with Stanford and become another of his lap dogs.

On September 12, 2004, after having met with Stanford and some of his minions, Spencer issued a statement that indicated the new government would be dealing with the Texan on a rather different playing field:

> My Government would have no problem looking at proposals from Mr. Allen Stanford for resort development in the North Sound area [where Stanford wanted to build his hangars and a tourist complex] once they are completely de-linked from the Asian Village deal; once his proposals respect the ecological integrity of the North Sound area; and once his proposals respect the dignity and the sovereignty of the Antiguan and Barbudan people.
>
> I think Mr. Stanford understands and respects these conditions. It is clear to me that the Antiguan and Barbudan people have had no option but to judge Mr. Stanford by the company he kept prior to March 23rd, 2004.
>
> Prior to March 23rd, Mr. Stanford dealt with a supine government that could not possibly have elicited anything but the

treatment that its members merited. It does not now appear to me that the gentleman described as the country's largest single investor has any difficulty working with members of a Government that looks him in the eye and bargains hard in the interest of the people.

It was the development of Guiana Island ("the Asian Village deal") that Spencer had acceded to a few weeks later, and then had reversed his decision, as mentioned in the Hangar Address. In fact, Spencer had pretty much thrown cold water on most of Stanford's grandiose plans. Even though Stanford tried to, well, persuade Spencer to go along with all his schemes by promising more "investments" and suspending payments on loans he had made to the government, including the debt from the new-hospital construction, Spencer held his ground.

Indeed, the considerable advantages of centering his financial empire in Antigua ultimately contributed to The Crash. Stanford's decision to move his operations to U.S. soil, to St. Croix, in 2007 was clearly intended to send a message to Baldwin Spencer: Play my way or I will take my marbles and go home.

Rumors arose that Spencer had truckled to Stanford, sobered by Stanford's power play. In the event, even if the rumors were true, it was too late. Thus the tough posture taken by the Spencer government was to prove irrelevant. The jobs disappeared along with Stanford. But at least Spencer could blame the entire mess on Lester Bird and the ALP, even though he was not without culpability himself.

Had Stanford built his financial Potemkin Village on, say, St. Croix in the first place, he would have been able to accomplish much of what he was attempting to pull off without the danger of a change in government dashing his plans. Stanford might have carried an Antigua passport, which he did (you can buy one for $40,000), but the Antigua government could still revoke it for cause. On American soil, Stanford would have been relatively untouchable. He could have had his offshore bank in Antigua and even kept the Bank of Antigua while being based in St. Croix. This is probably what he intended to do once he ran afoul of the Spencer administration. Again, it was far too late.

The precipitating factor in The Crash, to be sure, was the worldwide economic downturn beginning in the last quarter of 2008. Stanford's financial statements up until the crisis could, with considerable charity, be conceivably believed. But showing a solid gain while huge banks and insurance companies were going under, the stock market was tanking and the global economy was under siege, didn't add up – as Mr. Dalmady expertly pointed out.

In my purely layman's view, what Stanford's alleged book-cooking until late 2008 was doing was concealing his astonishingly lunatic investments and shameless lifestyle. When the recession hit, the manipulations *became* a Ponzi scheme.

Stanford is not so rash as to actually *intend* to get away with paying off old investors with new investors' money. He understands that road would lead to destruction. But because of the economic retraction, the Stanford Experience turned into a Ponzi operation all by itself. This is not to say that what Stanford was doing was defensible; it is to say, simply, that he fell directly into his own trap.

For those inclined to go into the financial-fraud business, they can learn much from the Stanford case. Here are some basic rules:

- *Make sure that as few people as possible know what you are actually doing.*

Stanford's "Board of Directors" comprised his father James, 82 years old; Stanford Financial Group CFO Jim Davis; and Oliver Goswick, a family acquaintance who was a used-car salesman and a cattle rancher, whose son Richard said, "He can't string seven words together" after a severe stroke in 2000.

The only people who actually knew the details were Davis and Allen Stanford.

- *Hire an auditor nobody ever heard of.*

Even though PricewaterhouseCoopers or KPMG, both reputable firms with offices in Antigua, could have been enlisted to check the SIB books, Stanford's auditor was an Antiguan, Charlesworth Hewlett, with few other clients, if any. He was the Stanford auditor for ten years. Six weeks before Stanford was initially charged, Hewlett died, at 72.

- *When the jig is up, blame everybody else.*

Stanford was quick to put any "irregularities" at the feet of his college-days friend Jim Davis. He blamed a broker in Houston for taking Mexican drug money. He blamed Baldwin Spencer for preventing him from developing Guiana Island. He blamed the SEC and the FBI for ruining his life. Caribbean Sun Airlines failed because of "increased overflying" of San Juan.

- *Pretend your investors' money is where it isn't.*

Some 80 percent of the Stanford investments were not in liquid assets like publicly traded equities, bonds, currencies, precious metals and so on. They were in real estate, private-equity deals, three silly movie ventures and rich-men's toys like private jet planes and swanky residences. And, of course, Stanford's pocket.

- *Dismiss doubts about your operation by calling former employees malcontents.*

While this is an old tried-and-true strategy, used by Enron and Tyco executives when they were fingered by former associates, it is remarkably effective still. Attack the motives and the messenger and buy some time.

- *Be prepared to give plenty of money to politicians.*

Stanford gave millions of dollars to political figures and ran a lobbying office out of Washington, D.C. These lobbying efforts were chiefly to keep offshore-banking laws as toothless as possible. Money went to both major parties, but mostly to Democrats, who Stanford considered more likely to be influenced and influential. He met Barack Obama when the President was a U.S. senator.

These basic rules are hardly exhaustive, but they will be useful in starting up your very own confidence game.

The irony of the Stanford Experience is that, like so many other promoters and snake-oil salesmen, the talents he was gifted with could have been applied to making money honestly, or at least legally. But Sir Allen's ego was too big to settle for earning a fortune using his resources and those of the people he hired, most of whom were capable if not always outstanding in their jobs. Stanford was unable to resist his basic narcissism, his need for attention and slobbering sycophants kowtowing to his elevated sense of superiority.

Stanford's self-celebration included, of course, his conspicuous philanthropy. He supported, quite generously in some cases, good causes, including St. Jude's Hospital and programs for Antiguan kids. But one has to suspect that this overt benevolence was a method, not a charitable impulse. Even his pal Lester Bird once remarked, "Mr. Stanford is not a philanthropist. He's a businessman."

Epilogue

As I write this, Sir R. Allen Stanford, Knight Commander of the Most Distinguished Order of the Nation, languishes in a federal lockup outside of Houston. Indications are his trial will take a year or more. His friend, or erstwhile friend, Jim Davis, is free on $500,000 bail and plans to plead guilty to all charges. Laura Pendergest-Holt, a woman in her 30s whom Davis met in church, somehow got sucked into the maelstrom of the Stanford Experience and faces a stint in prison, the last thing she could ever have imagined when she went to work for Stanford Financial Group. Former Antigua financial regulator Leroy King will be extradited to the United States where he will be charged with complicity in the scheme and with accepting bribes from Stanford. A handful of other Stanford executives have also been charged with a bagful of frauds and misrepresentations to the company's clients.

Civil lawsuits and possible criminal charges loom for dozens of independent brokers and CD peddlers who assured customers of the legitimacy of the Stanford International Bank. These criminal and civil proceedings will doubtless endure for years at huge expense and even greater personal tragedy for all concerned.

Our dear friend Keva Margetson was taken by cancer in 2008. Mona Quintyne, I am told, is struggling with a mental disorder. Many other people with whom we worked and played in Antigua have moved on with their lives, some happily, some not.

Left to twist in the wind are tens of thousands of folks, both rich and not so rich, who trusted their money – in some cases all their money – to the care of Sir Allen. Most will emerge with repayments of a few cents on the dollar when all the assets have been identified and liquidated. This will also take many years, a process that some will never see completed.

Antigua will suffer for decades, as its name has become a warning flag to offshore investors. Even tourists thinking of a Caribbean holiday will remember Antigua as the venue of Stanford's enormities and will dismiss the island as a corrupt and untrustworthy place, its name muddied by hosting what might be remembered as one of the biggest heists in history. The 15 or so remaining offshore banks there are being pummeled by nervous withdrawals and will continue to suffer under the detrimental halo effect of SIB's ignominious disintegration.

The *Antigua Sun,* inexplicably still publishing (I am told it is being subsidized by the Bank of Antigua, the commercial bank Stanford owned that was taken over by the Eastern Caribbean Central Bank), might survive under new ownership and arguably might prosper free of the political stain of having toadied to the Bird faction under Stanford's heavy hand. If the paper can stay afloat, we pray it will become the kind of media outlet we thought we could create and were prevented from realizing: an honest and persistent watchdog over the Antigua government and a source of disinterested commentary on issues important to the Antiguan people.

There are some people, not many, who believe that Sir Allen is innocent of all the accusations. As time goes on, this faith seems less and less plausible, although in America we cling, properly, to the presumption of innocence until a court of law finds otherwise. Cheating on your wife, lying to your friends, visiting injustices and cruelties on your employees, living in conspicuous luxury, devouring money on personal indulgences and making imprudent and even idiotic investments are not, *per se*, crimes under secular law.

There is, however, another judge in another place. And there is no lawyer on earth that can rescue any man from His terrible swift sword.

Appendix

Author's note: The following is the criminal indictment brought by a grand jury against Stanford et al.

SOUTHERN DISTRICT OF TEXAS
HOUSTON DIVISION
UNITED STATES OF AMERICA

June 18, 2009

INDICTMENT

The Grand Jury Charges:

COUNT ONE
Conspiracy to Commit Mail, Wire and Securities Fraud

1. Stanford Financial Group (SFG) was the parent company of Stanford International Bank, Ltd. and a web of other affiliated financial services entities, including Stanford Group Company. SFG maintained offices in several locations, including Houston, Texas, Memphis, Tennessee, and Miami, Florida.

2. Stanford International Bank, Ltd. (SIBL) was a private, offshore bank with offices on the island of Antigua and elsewhere. SIBL was organized in or about 1985 in Montserrat, originally under the name of Guardian

International Bank. In or about 1989, SIBL's principal banking location was moved to Antigua.

3. SIBL's primary investment product was marketed as a "Certificate of Deposit" (CD). SIBL marketed CDs to investors promising substantially higher rates of return than were generally offered at banks in the United States from 2001 to 2008. In its 2007 Annual Report to investors, SIBL purported to have approximately $6.7 billion worth of the CD deposits and over $7 billion in total assets. In its December 2000 Monthly Report, SIBL purported to have over 30,000 clients from 131 countries representing $8.5 billion in assets.

4. Stanford Group Company (SGC), a Houston-based company, was founded in or about 1995. SGC was registered with the Securities and Exchange Commission (SEC) as a broker-dealer and investment advisor. SGC was also a member of the Financial Industry Regulatory Agency, formerly the National Association of Securities Dealers, and the U.S. Securities Investor Protection Insurance Corporation (SIPIC). Although SGC and the financial advisers employed by SGC promoted the sale of SIBL's CDs through SGC's 25 offices located throughout the United States, SIBL's CDs were not insured by SIPIC or the Federal Deposit Insurance Corporation (FDIC).

5. In Antigua, SIBL was purportedly regulated by the Financial Services Regulatory Commission (FSRC), an agency of the Antiguan government, and was subject to annual on-site inspection by the FSRC. The FSRC claimed

on its website that it conducted these inspections to determine the solvency of the banks, review the quality of the investments, and review the accuracy of the banks' returns. Annually, SIBL provided to the FSRC an "Analysis of Investments" report which listed purported values for SIBL's investments. FSRC did not, however, audit SIBL's financial statements or verify the value SIBL ascribed to its investments in the Analysis of Investments.

6. Defendant Robert Allen Stanford controlled SFG and its affiliated companies, including, through a holding company, SIBL. STANFORD was the chairman of the SIBL Board of Directors and a member of SIBL's Investment Committee. STANFORD, among other things, received regular updates and financial reports on the investment activities of SIBL; made hiring decisions for SIBL; made decisions about what revenue and asset numbers to report to investors and others; made investment decisions for SIBL; updated investors and others about the activities and financial status of SIBL; and approved reports to investors and others about the financial condition of SIBL. STANFORD also authorized SIBL to make loans to himself and authorized SIBL to purchase property from STANFORD-controlled entities and to sell property to STANFORD-controlled entities.

7. JAMES M. DAVIS, a co-conspirator not named as a defendant herein, was the Chief Financial Officer (CFO) for SFG and SIBL, and served as a member of SIBL's Investment Committee. DAVIS, among other things, regularly consulted with STANFORD about the financial

status of SIBL, including investment decisions; received regular updates on SIBL's revenue and loss records; made decisions, based on the direction of STANFORD, about what revenue and asset numbers to report to investors and others; updated investors and others about the financial status and operations of SIBL; and approved reports to investors and others about the financial condition of SIBL.

8. Defendant LAURA PENDERGEST-HOLT was the Chief Investment Officer (CIO) of SFG. In or about December 2005, HOLT was appointed by the SIBL Board of Directors as a member of SIBL's Investment Committee. PENDERGEST-HOLT, among other things, held herself out to investors, employees of SIBL and SFG, and others as managing the entire investment portfolio of SIBL; updated investors and employees of SIBL and SFG regarding the financial status of SIBL; provided information about SIBL's investment portfolio to SFG and SGC financial brokers; and supervised SFG research analysts.

9. Defendant GILBERTO LOPEZ was the Chief Accounting Officer of SFG. LOPEZ, among other things, was responsible for tracking SIBL revenues, assets and liabilities, and was responsible for the preparation of the revenue and asset numbers used in SIBL's financial reports.

10. Defendant MARK KUHRT was the Global Controller for Stanford Financial Group Global Management, an affiliate of SFG and SIBL. KUHRT, among other things, maintained calculations of investment revenue of SIBL and, along with

LOPEZ, was responsible for the preparation of the revenue and asset numbers used in SIBL's financial reports.

11. Defendant LEROY KING was the Administrator and Chief Executive Officer for the FSRC. KING, among other things, was responsible for Antigua's regulatory oversight of SIBL's investment portfolio, including the review of SIBL financial reports for the Antiguan Government, and the response to requests by foreign regulators, including the SEC, for information and documents about SIBL's operations.

BACKGROUND
SIBL's Investment "Program"

12. STANFORD, HOLT, LOPEZ, KUHRT, DAVIS and others managed, marketed and monitored SIBL's CD investment program. The defendants and their conspirators caused investors and potential investors in SIBL CDs to receive a Disclosure Statement, amended several times over the years, and other documents providing information regarding SIBL, including data purportedly depicting SIBL's historical investment portfolio performance by specific categories of investment and updating SIBL investors on the financial condition of SIBL.

13. In promoting the SIBL CDs to investors, STANFORD, HOLT and DAVIS represented and caused others to represent: (a) the safety and security of SIBL's investments and CDs; (b) consistent double-digit returns on the bank's

investment portfolio; and (c) high return rates on the SIBL CDs that greatly exceeded those offered by commercial banks in the United States.

14. STANFORD, HOLT, LOPEZ, KUHRT, DAVIS, and others caused to be sent to investors Annual Reports purportedly representing SIBL's earnings from its "diversified investments." For example, the Annual Reports listed investment earnings of approximately $479 million in 2006, and approximately $642 million in 2007.

15. Commencing in or about 2000, STANFORD sought to increase sales of SIBL CDs in the United States. To do so, SGC recruited investment advisors, along with their clients, from other brokerage firms. Financial advisors at SGC would receive a 1% commission based upon the value of CDs they sold, and were eligible to receive additional commissions for CD sales. STANFORD, HOLT and DAVIS provided and caused to be provided information to these financial advisors about the financial condition of SIBL and the SIBL CDs.

16. SIBL investors and potential investors were not advised of the actual investments made by SIBL and could not determine the nature and risk of investments. Unknown to investors, the defendants and their conspirators internally segregated SIBL's investment portfolio into three investment tiers: (a) cash and cash equivalents ("Tier I"); (b) investments with "outside portfolio managers" ("Tier II"); and (c) other assets ("Tier III").

17. According to internal SIBL documents, as of June 30, 2008: Tier I investments represented only about 9% of the purported total value of SIBL's investments; Tier II investments represented only about 10% of the purported total value of SIBL's investments; and Tier III investments represented more than 80% of the purported total value of SIBL's investments.

18. SIBL's Treasurer ("the SIBL Treasurer") had primary responsibility for the Tier I cash and cash equivalent investments.

19. Unknown to investors, SGC financial advisors and others, HOLT "monitored" only Tier II investments, which were actually managed by well-known investment entities outside of SIBL that had complete discretion over the Tier II investments. SIBL would provide funds for investments to these "outside portfolio managers," also referred to as "money managers," and the money managers would select how funds would be invested for Tier II, that is, what investments would be made, limited by the funds available to them.

20. STANFORD and DAVIS directed, managed, and monitored the remaining investments – the Tier III investments. According to internal SIBL documents, as of June 30, 2008, these Tier III investments comprised the majority of the purported value of SIBL's investment portfolio. Approximately 50% of the purported value of Tier III (approximately $3.2 billion) included investments

in artificially valued real estate and approximately 30% of the purported value of Tier III (approximately $1.6 billion) included notes on personal loans to STANFORD. STANFORD, DAVIS and others did not disclose to, and actively concealed from, investors, SGC and SIBL employees, and others the fact that approximately $4.8 billion in purported Tier III investments consisted of such artificially valued real estate and notes on personal loans to STANFORD.

21. In its Monthly Report to investors for December 2008, SIBL reported total assets of over $8 billion, and an approximate 1.3% decline in earnings for the year, which the Monthly Report contrasted with the performance of other financial indices reporting approximately 30% to 40% declines. As set forth above, it was not disclosed in the Report that approximately $4.8 billion of the purported $8 billion "value" of these "total assets" was in notes on additional loans to STANFORD and in interests in certain "island properties," the values of which had been grossly overstated.

Marketing of SIBL CDs

22. STANFORD, HOLT, DAVIS, and others routinely made presentations to financial advisors employed by SGC regarding the financial condition of SIBL and its investment portfolio. The SGC financial advisors, in turn, provided information to prospective investors regarding the CD investment program.

23. STANFORD, HOLT, and DAVIS, at times, made presentations directly to individuals or groups of prospective investors regarding SIBL's CD program and to existing investors who were considering additional CD purchases or redemptions of their CDs.

24. STANFORD regularly sponsored "Top Producers Club" (TPC) meetings, which were held at various locations, including January 2009 meetings in Phoenix and Miami, and were attended by financial advisors and others. At these TPC meetings, STANFORD, HOLT, DAVIS and others touted the purported economic condition and viability of SIBL to instill confidence in the CD investment program and encourage the financial advisors to aggressively market and sell SIBL's CDs.

25. STANFORD, HOLT, DAVIS and others, on behalf of SIBL, reviewed and caused the issuance of SIBL's periodic Annual, Quarterly and Monthly Reports, which were provided to investors and used by SGC's financial advisers in marketing SIBL's CDs. In marketing the CDs as safe and secure investments, the financial advisors and SIBL's brochures, reports and other documents variously emphasized that SIBL was "strong, safe and fiscally sound" and that its investment strategy was a "conservative approach" and "long term, hands on and globally diversified with strong liquidity and minimal leverage."

SEC Investigation

26. In or about 2005, the Securities and Exchange Commission (SEC) initiated an investigation of SFG and began making official inquiries with the FSRC regarding the value and content of SIBL's purported investments.

27. In June 2005, the SEC confidentially requested the assistance of KING at the FSRC in determining whether SIBL and SFG had "perpetrated a fraud upon investors."

28. In September 2006, the SEC confidentially requested from KING at the FSRC, among other things, copies of "the FSRC's exam reports" regarding SIBL.

29. In or about January 2009, the SEC issued subpoenas to STANFORD, HOLT and DAVIS seeking both testimony and documents regarding SIBL's investment portfolio.

30. In late January 2009, the SEC notified SIBL's attorney that the SEC had scheduled sworn testimony of the SIBL President and HOLT to provide "credible and verifiable testimony regarding all of the assets" of SIBL.

31. On or about February 10, 2009, HOLT attended an SEC proceeding in Fort Worth, Texas, and provided sworn testimony to the SEC regarding SIBL's investment portfolio.

32. On or about February 16, 2009, the SEC filed a Complaint seeking emergency relief against SFG and

related individuals and entities in the United States District Court for the Northern District of Texas ("the District Court"), alleging a "massive, on-going fraud." In its Amended Complaint, filed February 27, 2009, the SEC further alleged "misappropriation of billions of dollars of investor funds" and other fraudulent conduct.

33. On or about February 17, 2009, the District Court appointed an individual – known as a Receiver – to take over SFG and its related entities to protect and preserve their investments and assets.

THE CONSPIRACY

34. From in or about at least September 1999, through on or about February 17, 2009, in the Southern District of Texas and elsewhere, the defendants, ROBERT ALLEN STANFORD, LAURA PENDERGEST-HOLT. GILBERTO LOPEZ, MARK KUHRT and LEROY KING, did willfully, that is, with the intent to further the objects of the conspiracy, and knowingly combine, conspire, confederate and agree with each other, with JAMES M. DAVIS, and with others, known and unknown to the Grand Jury, to commit certain offenses against the United States, that is:

(a) to devise and intend to devise a scheme and artifice to defraud, and to obtain money and property by means of materially false and fraudulent pretenses, representations and promises, knowing that they were false and fraudulent when made, and causing to be delivered certain mail matter by the United States Postal Service and any private or commercial interstate carrier, according to the directions thereon, for the purpose of executing the scheme, in violation of Title 18, United States Code, Section 1341;

(b) to devise and intend to devise a scheme and artifice to defraud, and to obtain money and property by means of materially false and fraudulent pretenses, representations and promises, knowing that they were false and fraudulent when made, and transmitting and causing to be transmitted certain wire communications in interstate and foreign commerce, for the purpose of executing the scheme, in violation of Title 18, United States Code, Section 1343; and

(c) to, by use of the means and instrumentalities of interstate commerce, the mails, and wire communications, directly and indirectly, use and employ manipulative and deceptive devices and contrivances in connection with the purchase and sale of securities, that is, certificates of deposit of the Stanford International Bank, Ltd. and in connection with such transactions, (i) employ devices, schemes, and artifices to defraud holders of the securities; (ii) make untrue statements of material facts and omit to state material facts necessary in order to make the statements made, in the light of the circumstances under which they were made, not misleading; and (iii) engage in acts, practices, and courses of business which operated and would operate as a fraud and deceit upon holders of securities, in violation of Title 15, United States Code,

Sections 78j(b) and 78f(a), and Title 17, Code of Federal Regulations, Section 240.10b-5.

PURPOSE OF THE CONSPIRACY

35. It was a purpose of the conspiracy that the defendants and their conspirators would solicit and obtain billions of dollars of investors' funds through false pretenses, representations and promises, all in order to obtain substantial economic benefits for themselves and others through the payment of fees, wages, bonuses, and other monies, and unauthorized diversions, misuse, and misappropriation of funds.

MANNER AND MEANS OF THE CONSPIRACY

The manner and means by which the defendants and their conspirators sought to accomplish the objects and purpose of the conspiracy included, among other things, the following:

36. It was a part of the conspiracy that the defendants and their conspirators would make and cause to be made false and misleading representations in promotional materials, periodic reports, newsletters, emails sent by mail and wire transmissions in interstate commerce to investors and others, and in conversations, presentations and meetings with investors and others, including the following:

False Statements Regarding the Value of SIBL's Finances:

a. The defendants and their conspirators would make and cause to be made false and misleading representations concerning SIBL's financial condition touting year-by-year percentage and dollar amount increases in the purported value of its earnings, revenue, and assets, including an increase in the purported value of SIBL's assets from approximately $1.2 billion in 2001 to approximately $8.5 billion in December 2008, when, in truth and in fact, those values were false and designed to deceive investors into believing that SIBL's "investments" were performing as falsely touted.

b. The defendants and their conspirators would make and cause to be made false and misleading representations concerning SIBL's investment strategy as seeking to "minimize risk and achieve liquidity," when, in truth and in fact, approximately 80% of SIBL's investment portfolio consisted of illiquid investments, such as (i) grossly overvalued real and personal property that SIBL had acquired from STANFORD-controlled entities through fraudulent "round trip" transactions and (ii) unsecured notes on more than a billion dollars in personal loans to STANFORD.

False Statements Regarding the Management of Investors' Funds:

c. STANFORD, HOLT, DAVIS and others would make false and misleading misrepresentations that SIBL's entire investment portfolio was closely and well-managed, including identifying HOLT as SFG's "Chief Investment Officer" and as a member of SIBL's "Investment Committee," responsible for management of SIBL's entire portfolio of assets through a "global network" of "outside portfolio managers" and "money managers," when, in truth and in fact, HOLT ultimately "managed" less than approximately 10% of SIBL's investment portfolio.

d. STANFORD, KING, DAVIS and others would make false and misleading representations regarding the nature and extent of regulatory oversight of SIBL, including that SIBL's operations and financial condition were being scrutinized by the FSRC in Antigua and that SIBL's financial statements were subject to annual audits and regulatory inspections by Antiguan regulators, when, in truth and in fact, STANFORD had made corrupt payments to KING in order to ensure that the FSRC did not accurately audit SIBL's financial statements or verify the existence or value of SIBL's assets as reflected in the SIBL financial statements.

37. It was further a part of the conspiracy that the defendants and their conspirators would create and cause to be created false and misleading accounting books and records and other documents concerning the financial condition and investment portfolio of SIBL, through, among other things, the following means:

a. The defendants and their conspirators would create false books and records containing artificial values for SIBL's investment portfolio and its return on investment by causing already inflated values that had been reported to investors for prior periods to be adjusted (multiplied) by a percentage increase "as deemed necessary" to produce the new false investment and revenue values.

b. The defendants and their conspirators would conceal and disguise as "investments" in SIBL's books and records, and fail to disclose in such books and records, that STANFORD had received and not repaid more than a billion dollars of personal loans from SIBL.

c. The defendants and their conspirators would conceal and disguise in SIBL's books and records fraudulent "round trip" transactions in which SIBL would transfer interests in real and personal property to STANFORD-controlled entities and then back to SIBL at grossly inflated values, in order to mask the artificially inflated values of those "assets" on SIBL's books and records, to falsely disguise and purportedly "settle" a substantial portion of the loans STANFORD had taken from SIBL, and to falsely inflate the value and disguise the nature of STANFORD'S purported capital contributions to SIBL.

38. It was further a part of the conspiracy that STANFORD would make regular secret corrupt payments of thousands of dollars in cash to KING, the Administrator and CEO of the FSRC, to ensure that, among other things:

a. The FSRC would not exercise its true regulatory functions in verifying the existence and value of SIBL's investments;

b. KING corruptly would provide to STANFORD, DAVIS and others information about official inquiries that the FSRC had received from United States regulators who had requested information from the FSRC regarding "possible fraud perpetrated upon investors" by SIBL; and

c. KING would make false representations in response to official inquiries of regulators, including U.S. regulators, and would seek and receive the assistance of STANFORD, DAVIS and others, in preparing false responses to such inquiries.

39. It was further a part of the conspiracy that STANFORD, HOLT, DAVIS and others, would conceal from the SEC the true operations and financial condition of SIBL, and the true nature and value of its holdings, and would forestall the SEC's investigation through various means, including, among others, the following:

a. STANFORD, HOLT, DAVIS and others would make and cause to be made false and misleading statements to SEC attorneys in order to persuade them to delay the sworn testimony of STANFORD and DAVIS by falsely representing that HOLT and SIBL's President could better explain specific details about SIBL's entire investment portfolio and assets rather than STANFORD and DAVIS; and

b. HOLT would attend the SEC proceeding in Fort Worth, Texas, on February 10, 2009, at which HOLT would provide false sworn testimony regarding SIBL's investment portfolio, her knowledge of the portfolio, and her preparation for her testimony.

OVERT ACTS

In furtherance of the conspiracy and to achieve the objects and purpose thereof, at least one of the conspirators committed and caused to be committed, in the Southern District of Texas and elsewhere, at least one of the following overt acts, among others:

40. In or about April 2000, STANFORD and DAVIS caused to be sent to investors SIBL's Annual Report for 1999, which included representations that SIBL's total assets at year end 1999 were up 28.75% to $675.89 million, with a $3.81 million profit.

41. In or about April 2001, STANFORD and DAVIS caused to be sent to investors SIBL's Annual Report for 2000, which included representations that SIBL's total assets at year end 2000 were up 22.84% to $830.70 million, with profit up 31.61% to $5.01 million.

42. In or about April 2002, STANFORD and DAVIS caused to be sent to investors SIBL's Annual Report for 2001, which included representations that SIBL's total assets at

year end 2001 were up 44.19% to $ 1.198 billion, with a "record" profit up 142.59% to $12.16 million.

43. In or about April 2003, STANFORD and DAVIS caused to be sent to investors SIBL's Annual Report for 2002, which included representations that SIBL's total assets at year end 2002 were up 43.1% to $1.7 billion, with a "record operating profit" up 97.9% to $23.7 million, and which included a "Report of Management" signed by STANFORD and DAVIS representing that the financial statements presented "fairly and consistently the Bank's financial position and results of operations."

44. In or about March 2004, STANFORD and DAVIS caused to be sent to investors SIBL's Annual Report for 2003,which included representations that SIBL's total assets at year end 2003 were up 29.9% to $2.2 billion, with a "record operating profit" up 39.7% to $33.1 million, and which included a "Report of Management" signed by STANFORD and DAVIS.

45. On or about February 7, 2005, KING caused a deposit to be made in the amount of approximately $15,000 in U.S. currency into a bank account he controlled in Tucker, Georgia.

46. On or about February 25, 2005, KING caused a deposit to be made in the amount of approximately $9,000 in U.S. currency into a bank account he controlled in Tucker, Georgia.

47. In or about March 2005, STANFORD and DAVIS caused to be sent to investors and placed on SIBL's website SIBL's Annual Report for 2004, which included representations that SIBL's total assets at year end 2004 were up 38.7% to $3.1 billion, with a "fifth consecutive year of record operating profit, reaching $36.2 million," and which also included a "Report of Management" signed by STANFORD and DAVIS.

48. On or about March 24, 2005, KING caused a deposit to be made in the amount of approximately $9,700 in U.S. currency into a bank account he controlled in Tucker, Georgia.

49. On or about June 21, 2005, KING represented in a letter to the SEC that if STANFORD were running a Ponzi scheme then the FSRC's examination of SIBL would have detected it, even though KING knew that, at his direction, the FSRC was not scrutinizing SIBL's operations and finances.

50. On or about December 30, 2005, KING caused a deposit to be made in the amount of approximately $6,000 in U.S. currency into a bank account he controlled in Tucker, Georgia.

51. In or about March 2006, STANFORD and DAVIS caused to be sent to investors and placed on SIBL's website SIBL's Annual Report for 2005, which included representations that SIBL's total assets at year end 2005 were up 31.5 % to $4.1 billion, with "operating profit" of $35.9 million, "slightly down" from the 2004 "record profit" of $36.2

million, and which also included a "Report of Management" signed by STANFORD and DAVIS.

52. On or about March 10, 2006, KING caused deposits to be made in the total amount of approximately $9,800 in U.S. currency into bank accounts he controlled in Tucker, Georgia.

53. On or about March 14, 2006, KING caused a deposit to be made in the amount of approximately $7,000 in U.S. currency into a bank account he controlled in Acworth, Georgia.

54. On or about March 20, 2006, KING caused a deposit to be made in the amount of approximately $8,000 in U.S. currency into a bank account he controlled in Decatur, Georgia.

55. On or about March 27, 2006, KING caused a deposit to be made in the amount of approximately $5,000 in U.S. currency into a bank account he controlled in Acworth, Georgia.

56. On or about August 31, 2006, KING caused deposits to be made in the total amount of approximately $2,000 in U.S. currency into a bank account he controlled in Chamblee, Georgia.

57. On or about September 18, 2006, KING caused a deposit to be made in the amount of approximately $5,000

in U.S. currency into a bank account he controlled in Tucker, Georgia.

58. On or about September 21, 2006, KING caused a deposit to be made in the amount of approximately $6,000 in U.S. currency into a bank account he controlled in Chamblee, Georgia.

59. On or about September 25, 2006, KING delivered to STANFORD and DAVIS official correspondence which the FSRC had received from the SEC.

60. On or about September 25, 2006, STANFORD, KING and DAVIS had a conversation in which they discussed how to respond to an SEC request for information about SIBL.

61. On or about September 28, 2006, KING caused a deposit to be made in the amount of approximately $6,000 in U.S. currency into a bank account he controlled in Tucker, Georgia.

62. On or about October 10, 2006, KING provided to the SEC an official response of the FSRC regarding SIBL, which response contained text actually prepared by STANFORD and others.

63. On or about October 23, 2006, KING caused a deposit to be made in the amount of approximately $8,000 in U.S. currency into a bank account he controlled in Tucker, Georgia.

64. On or about January 11, 2007, KUHRT sent an email from Houston, Texas, to DAVIS in Tupelo, Mississippi, with a copy to LOPEZ in Houston, Texas, attaching an artificial SIBL revenue entry for December 2006 and noting that the SIBL President was looking for financials that he could present at an upcoming Top Producers Club event.

65. On or about January 31, 2007, KING caused a deposit to be made in the amount of approximately $4,000 in U.S. currency into a bank account he controlled in Tucker, Georgia.

66. On or about March 19, 2007, KING caused a deposit to be made in the amount of approximately $6,000 in U.S. currency into a bank account he controlled in Hallandale, Florida.

67. In or about April 2007, STANFORD and DAVIS caused to be sent to investors and placed on SIBL's website SIBL's Annual Report for 2006, which included representations that SIBL's total assets at year end 2006 were up 31.5% to $5.3 billion, with an "operating profit of $28.8 million," and which also included a Report of Management signed by STANFORD and DAVIS.

68. On or about April 16, 2007, KUHRT sent an email from Houston, Texas, to DAVIS in Tupelo, Mississippi, with a copy to LOPEZ, in Houston, Texas, which attached a falsely inflated March 2007 revenue entry for SIBL.

69. On or about April 16, 2007, KING caused a deposit to be made in the amount of approximately $9,000 in U.S. currency into a bank account he controlled in Chamblee, Georgia.

70. In or about June 2007, STANFORD, HOLT, and DAVIS caused a newsletter, called the Stanford Eagle, to be sent to investors in which representations were made that SFG had "worldwide assets under management or advisement" exceeding $43 billion and which touted the "Stanford Investment Model" as one in which they would "carefully consider asset classes, investment strategies, sectors and regions of the world that most investors either don't have easy access to or rarely get information about."

71. On or about September 14, 2007, KING caused a deposit to be made in the amount of approximately $5,500 in U.S. currency into a bank account he controlled in Tucker, Georgia.

72. On or about December 24, 2007, KING caused a deposit to be made in the amount of approximately $4,470 in U.S. currency into a bank account he controlled in Tucker, Georgia.

73. On or about January 23, 2008, KING caused a withdrawal to be made in the amount of approximately $15,000 from a bank account he controlled in New York, New York and deposited the money into an investment account in New York.

74. On or about January 30, 2008, KING caused a deposit to be made in the amount of approximately $9,500 in U.S. currency into a bank account he controlled in Tucker, Georgia.

75. On or about March 10, 2008, DAVIS sent a fax to KUHRT concerning creation of false revenue entries for SIBL and instructing KUHRT to reduce equities and increase fixed income.

76. In or about April 2008, STANFORD and DAVIS caused to be sent to investors SIBL's Annual Report for 2007, which included representations that SIBL's total assets grew by 32.3% to $7.1 billion and that SIBL earned a "record operating profit of $43.6 million," and which also included a Report of Management signed by STANFORD and DAVIS.

77. On or about April 8, 2008, KUHRT caused an SFG employee to send a fax from Houston, Texas, to DAVIS in Tupelo, Mississippi, which sought DAVIS' review and approval of false amounts to insert in the monthly report for SIBL's "Return on Investment" for March 2008, and asked what figures to reduce with the understanding that year-to-date income "should be about $1.8 million loss."

78. On or about April 8, 2008, DAVIS caused a reply fax to be sent from Tupelo, Mississippi, back to an SFG employee in Houston, Texas, titled: "SIBL Accrual for Approval MAR 2008," in which DAVIS provided hand-written instructions

regarding the need to "reduce equity" to "come in line with" a $1.8M loss.

79. On or about April 23, 2008, KING caused a deposit to be made in the amount of approximately $9,600 in U.S. currency into a bank account he controlled in Chamblee, Georgia.

80. On or about June 30, 2008, KING caused a deposit to be made in the amount of approximately $7,000 in U.S. currency into a bank account he controlled in Chamblee, Georgia.

81. In or about July 2008, STANFORD caused SIBL to sell interests in "island properties" to an entity controlled by STANFORD, which interests SIBL had acquired in 2008 for approximately $63.5 million.

82. In or about September and November 2008, STANFORD transferred interests in these "island properties" back to SIBL at a purported value of approximately $3.2 billion, a portion of which was than purportedly used to settle loans made by SIBL to STANFORD and as "capital contributions" of STANFORD to SIBL.

83. In or about fall 2008, STANFORD, KUHRT, LOPEZ, KING and DAVIS caused bogus reports to be provided to the FSRC and investors falsely representing the value of SIBL's total investments and including specific entries

establishing grossly inflated values for real estate purportedly held by SIBL.

84. On or about October 8, 2008, KUHRT caused an SFG employee to send a fax from St. Croix, U.S. Virgin Islands, to DAVIS, concerning "SIBL Accrual for Approval/SEPTEMBER 2008 ADDENDUM," and containing false revenue entries.

85. On or about October 28, 2008, HOLT sent an email to an SFG employee in which HOLT represented that there had been "no loss on the portfolio," that "a $235 million capital infusion was just made, "and that the liquidity stood at $1.5 billion."

86. On or about November 10, 2008, KUHRT sent an email from St. Croix, U.S. Virgin Islands, to DAVIS in Tupelo, Mississippi, with a copy to LOPEZ in Houston, Texas, which attached various fabricated Return on Investment scenarios for SIBL.

87. In or about December 2008, STANFORD, HOLT, DAVIS and others caused to be sent to investors in Houston, Texas, and elsewhere SIBL's Monthly Report for December 2008, which falsely represented that SIBL had received a "capital infusion" of approximately $541 million from STANFORD.

88. On or about December 8, 2008, KING caused a deposit to be made in the amount of approximately $6,800 in U.S.

currency into a bank account he controlled in Miami, Florida.

89. On or about December 11, 2008, KUHRT caused an SFG employee to send a fax from St. Croix, U.S. Virgin Islands, to DAVIS in Tupelo, Mississippi, regarding the "SIBL Accrual for Approval NOVEMBER 2008," which provided a false adjustment to show a small loss to deflect scrutiny of SIBL's records.

90. On or about December 23, 2008, LOPEZ, KUHRT and others caused a spreadsheet to be created outlining the "sale" and grossly inflated "valuation" of the island properties.

91. On or about December 24, 2008, KING caused a deposit to be made in the amount of approximately $4,200 in U.S. currency into a bank account he controlled in Tucker, Georgia.

92. On or about January 5, 2009, KUHRT caused an email to be sent from St. Croix, U.S. Virgin Islands, to LOPEZ in Houston, Texas, which attached a spreadsheet concerning an artificial "round trip" real estate transaction to transfer interests in real estate back to SIBL.

93. On or about January 10, 2009, STANFORD, HOLT, DAVIS and others made presentations at a Top Producers Club meeting in Miami, Florida, at which they falsely touted the state of SIBL's investments and financial condition.

94. On or about January 16, 2009, STANFORD, HOLT, DAVIS and others made presentations at a Top Producers Club meeting in Phoenix, Arizona, at which they falsely touted the state of SIBL's investments and financial condition.

95. On or about January 21, 2009, at a meeting at STANFORD'S aircraft hangar in Miami, Florida, STANFORD, HOLT, DAVIS and others discussed how to respond to subpoenas that had been issued by the SEC in connection with an on-going investigation.

96. In or about January 2009, DAVIS instructed SIBL's Treasurer to destroy SIBL records which had been moved to Antigua.

97. On or about January 22, 2009, at a meeting with SEC attorneys at a restaurant in Houston, Texas, SIBL's attorney represented to the SEC attorneys that SIBL was "not a criminal enterprise" and that "all assets are there."

98. On or about January 23, 2009, at a meeting between SIBL's attorney and an SEC attorney at SFG's offices in Houston, Texas, SIBL's attorney requested that the SEC attorney defer the SEC subpoenas to STANFORD and DAVIS, and represented that HOLT and the SIBL President would be better witnesses than STANFORD and DAVIS, whom SIBL's attorney claimed were executive level officers of the company not involved in the "nuts and

bolts," and who could not tell the SEC attorneys about details of the bank's assets.

99. On or about January 24, 2009, SIBL's attorney sent an email to an SFG employee, forwarded on or about January 25, 2009, from the SFG employee to HOLT, DAVIS and others, with a copy to STANFORD, in which SIBL's attorney stated that he had persuaded the SEC that HOLT and the SIBL President would be better witnesses to testify about SIBL's entire portfolio of assets and stated that HOLT would "have to get up to speed on Tier 3."

100. On or about January 27, 2009, SIBL's attorney sent an email to HOLT and SIBL's President, with a copy to DAVIS and an SFG employee, regarding the need to address all three tiers of the SIBL asset portfolio, stating that they needed to "rise to the occasion" and that "our livelihood depends on it."

101. On or about February 4, 2009, HOLT, DAVIS and others met in Miami, Florida, and discussed the SEC testimony of HOLT and the SIBL President, STANFORD'S recent capital contribution to SIBL, SIBL's purported substantial investment in real estate, and SIBL's unsecured loans to STANFORD.

102. On or about February 4, 2009, at the Miami meeting, HOLT suggested that she only disclose in her testimony to the SEC the June 30, 2008 SFG financials as those numbers "looked better."

103. On or about February 10, 2009, prior to HOLT's testimony before the SEC, DAVIS spoke by telephone with HOLT regarding her planned testimony at the SEC proceeding.

104. On or about February 10, 2009, HOLT and SIBL's attorney attended an SEC proceeding in Fort Worth, Texas, at which HOLT provided sworn testimony to the SEC in which she (1) did not disclose the Miami meetings to prepare her testimony; and (2) represented that she did not know specifically the nature and allocation of assets in Tier III.

105. On or about February 11, 2009, HOLT caused funds in the amount of approximately $4.3 million to be sent by wire transfer from the Bank of New York to SIBL's operating account at the Bank of Houston in Houston, Texas.

106. On or about February 11, 2009, STANFORD caused a letter, addressed "Dear Client," to be sent to investors, in which STANFORD made representations that SIBL "remains a strong institution" and that he had "already added two capital infusions into the bank."

107. On or about February 12, 2009, STANFORD sent an email to SFG global employees, including employees in Houston, Texas, in which STANFORD made representations that SIBL "remained a strong institution" and that he had made "two recent capital infusions" into SIBL.

108. On or about February 13, 2009, HOLT caused funds in the amount of approximately $170,177 to be sent by wire transfer from the Bank of New York to SIBL's operating account at the Bank of Houston in Houston, Texas.

109. On or about February 17, 2009, at a meeting with SEC attorneys in Memphis, Tennessee, HOLT represented to the SEC attorneys that if she "knew anything about Tier III" she would tell them.

110. The acts alleged in Counts 2 through 18 of the Indictment are re-alleged and incorporated herein as additional overt acts in furtherance of the conspiracy and to achieve the objects and purpose thereof, all in violation of Title 18, United States Code, Section 371.